to

_____

from

_____

2minutes
A DAY

100 DEVOTIONALS

SELF-ESTEEM

about respecting yourself

*The quoted ideas expressed in this book (but not scripture verses) are not, in all cases, exact quotations, as
some have been edited for clarity and brevity. In all cases, the author has attempted to maintain the speaker's
original intent. In some cases, quoted material for this book was obtained from secondary sources, primarily
print media. While every effort was made to ensure the accuracy of these sources, the accuracy cannot be
guaranteed. For additions, deletions, corrections or clarifications in future editions of this text, please write
FAMILY CHRISTIAN PRESS.*

Scripture quotations are taken from:

The Holy Bible, King James Version

The Holy Bible, New International Version (NIV) Copyright © 1973, 1978, 1984, by International
Bible Society. Used by permission of Zondervan Publishing House. All rights reserved.

The New American Standard Bible®, (NASB) Copyright © 1960, 1962, 1963, 1968, 1971, 1972,
1973, 1975, 1977, 1995 by The Lockman Foundation. Used by permission.

The Holy Bible, New King James Version (NKJV) Copyright © 1982 by Thomas Nelson, Inc. Used
by permission.

The Holy Bible, New Living Translation, (NLT) Copyright © 1996. Used by permission of Tyndale
House Publishers, Inc., Wheaton, Illinois 60189. All rights reserved.

New Century Version®. (NCV) Copyright © 1987, 1988, 1991 by Word Publishing, a division of
Thomas Nelson, Inc. All rights reserved. Used by permission.

The Holy Bible: Revised Standard Version (RSV). Copyright 1946, 1952, 1959, 1973 by the
Division of Christian Education of the National Council of the Churches of Christ in the United
States of America. All rights reserved. Used by permission.

The Holy Bible, The Living Bible (TLB), Copyright © 1971 owned by assignment by Illinois
Regional Bank N.A. (as trustee). Used by permission of Tyndale House Publishers, Inc., Wheaton,
Illinois 60189. All rights reserved.

The Message (MSG) This edition issued by contractual arrangement with NavPress, a division of
The Navigators, U.S.A. Originally published by NavPress in English as THE MESSAGE: The Bible
in Contemporary Language copyright 2002-2003 by Eugene Peterson. All rights reserved.

The Holman Christian Standard Bible™ (HOLMAN CSB) Copyright © 1999, 2000, 2001 by Holman
Bible Publishers. Used by permission.

Cover Design by Kim Russell / Wahoo Designs
Page Layout by Bart Dawson

ISBN 1-58334-356-3

Printed in the United States of America

100 DEVOTIONALS

SELF-ESTEEM

Introduction

Can you spare two minutes each day for God? Of course you can . . . and of course you should! Scottish-born evangelist Henry Drummond correctly observed, "Ten minutes spent in Christ's company every day—even two minutes—will make the whole day different." How true. If you dedicate even a few minutes each morning to devotional reading and prayer, you will change the tone and direction of your life.

This book offers 100 quick devotionals about building self-esteem, and if you're like most folks on the planet, your self-esteem could stand a little tune-up from time to time. Maybe you want to look a certain way, act a certain way, or "fit in" with a certain peer group. Maybe you want to be "as perfect as possible," but you just don't think you're measuring up. And maybe, just maybe, when you fail to live up to your own impossible-to-meet standards, you beat yourself up . . . which results in lower self-esteem.

This book provides you with time tested principles for loving yourself more while beating yourself up less. The lessons on these pages are intended to teach you that you don't have to be perfect to be fabulous. So during the next 100 days, read a chapter each day and take each day's message to heart. Hopefully, by the time you get to the end of the book, you'll have a better understanding—and a greater appreciation—for the person who stares back at you each time you look in the mirror. When you do, God will smile . . . and so will the face in the mirror!

God Loves You
(and You Should, Too)

The unfailing love of the LORD never ends!
LAMENTATIONS 3:22 NLT

Face it: sometimes it can be tough to respect yourself, especially if you're feeling like a less-than-perfect citizen living in a world that seems to demand perfection. But before you go headlong into the self-criticism mode, think about this: God knows all your imperfections, all your faults, and all your shortcomings . . . and He loves you anyway. And because God loves you, you can—and should—feel good about the person you see when you look into the mirror.

If you've ever had the feeling that you simply don't "measure up," perhaps you've been measuring yourself by society's standards, not God's. If so, it's time to start worrying less about impressing other people and more about pleasing God. Starting now.

more stuff to think about

I am convinced our hearts are not healthy until they have
been satisfied by the only completely healthy love that exists:
the love of God Himself.

BETH MOORE

God loves you and wants you to experience
peace and life—abundant and eternal.

BILLY GRAHAM

God carries your picture in his wallet.

TONY CAMPOLO

The Big Idea

God's love makes everything look a lot better: When you
invite the love of God into your heart, everything in the world
looks different, including you.

SELF-ESTEEM

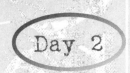

Put God First

*Jesus answered, "'Love the Lord your God
with all your heart, all your soul, and all your mind.'
This is the first and most important command."*
MATTHEW 22:37-38 NCV

Self-respect, like every other good thing in this universe, starts with God. In other words, you can't have a healthy relationship with yourself until you have a healthy relationship with God.

As you think about the nature of your relationship with God, remember this: you will always have some type of relationship with Him—it is inevitable that your life must be lived in relationship to God. The question is not *if* you will have a relationship with Him; the burning question is whether or not that relationship will be one that seeks to honor Him.

Are you willing to place God first in your life? And, are you willing to welcome God's Son into your heart? Unless you can honestly answer these questions with a resounding yes, then your relationship with God isn't what it could be or should be. Thankfully, God is always available, He's always ready to forgive, and He's waiting to hear from you now. The rest, of course, is up to you.

more stuff to think about

Give God what's right—not what's left!

ANONYMOUS

Jesus challenges you and me to keep our focus daily
on the cross of His will if we want to be His disciples.

ANNE GRAHAM LOTZ

Whatever you love most, be it sports, pleasure,
business or God, that is your god.

BILLY GRAHAM

The Big Idea

Today, spend a few minutes thinking about your relationship
with God. Is it really an intimate one-on-one connection,
or are you allowing other things to come between you and
your Creator? Write down three specific steps that you can
take right now to forge a stronger bond with your Heavenly
Father.

SELF-ESTEEM

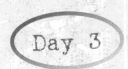
Don't Settle for Second, Third, or Fourth Best

But as for you, be strong and do not give up,
for your work will be rewarded.

2 CHRONICLES 15:7 NIV

Do you believe that you deserve the best, and that you can achieve the best? Or have you convinced yourself that you're a second-tier talent who'll be lucky to finish far back in the pack? Before you answer that question, remember this: God sent His Son so that you might enjoy the abundant life that Jesus describes in the familiar words of John 10:10. But, God's gifts are not guaranteed—it's up to you to claim them.

As you plan for the next stage of your life's journey, promise yourself that when it comes to the important things in life, you won't settle for second best. And what, pray tell, are the "important things"? Your faith, your family, your health, and your relationships, for starters. In each of these areas, you deserve to be a rip-roaring, top-drawer success.

So, if you want to achieve the best that life has to offer, convince yourself that you have the ability to earn the rewards you desire. Become sold on yourself—sold on your opportunities, sold on your potential, sold on your abilities. If you're sold on yourself, chances are, the world will soon become sold, too, and the results will be beautiful.

more stuff to think about

If, in your working hours, you make the work your end,
you will presently find yourself all unawares inside
the only circle in your profession that really matters.
You will be one of the sound craftsmen,
and other sound craftsmen will know it.

C. S. LEWIS

Few things fire up a person's commitment
like dedication to excellence.

JOHN MAXWELL

We are always making an offering.
If we do not give to God, we give to the devil.

VANCE HAVNER

The Big Idea

Don't "settle" for less: too many people find it is easy to
"settle" for second-best, third-best, one millionth-best, or
somewhere in between. Don't make that mistake. Ask God
for the courage, the perseverance, and the wisdom to select
the "first-best" path for you, and don't settle for anything less.

SELF-ESTEEM

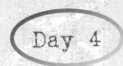

Learn to Think Optimistically About Yourself and Your Life

But if we look forward to something we don't have yet,
we must wait patiently and confidently.

ROMANS 8:25 NLT

Are you an optimist or a pessimist? The answer to this question will determine, to a surprising extent, how you feel about yourself.

As you look at the landscape of your life, do you see opportunities, possibilities, and blessings, or do you focus, instead, upon the more negative scenery? Do you spend more time counting your blessings or your misfortunes? If you've acquired the unfortunate habit of focusing too intently upon the negative aspects of your life, then your spiritual vision is in need of correction.

The way that you choose to view the scenery around you will have a profound impact on the quality, the tone, and the direction of your life. The more you focus on the beauty that surrounds you, the more beautiful your own life becomes.

more stuff to think about

Christ can put a spring in your step and
a thrill in your heart. Optimism and cheerfulness
are products of knowing Christ.

BILLY GRAHAM

We may run, walk, stumble, drive, or fly,
but let us never lose sight of the reason for the journey,
or miss a chance to see a rainbow on the way.

GLORIA GAITHER

Do not build up obstacles in your imagination.
Difficulties must be studied and dealt with,
but they must not be magnified by fear.

NORMAN VINCENT PEALE

The Big Idea

If you think you can do something, you probably can. If you
think you can't do something, you probably can't. That's why
it's so important to believe in yourself.

SELF-ESTEEM

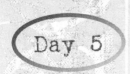

Day 5

Focus on the Right Stuff

Keep your eyes focused on what is right,
and look straight ahead to what is good.

PROVERBS 4:25 NCV

In the busyness and confusion of daily life, it is easy to lose focus, and it is easy to become frustrated. We are imperfect human beings struggling to manage our lives as best we can, but we often fall short. When we are distracted or disappointed, we may neglect to share a kind word or a kind deed. This oversight hurts others, but it hurts us most of all.

Today, slow yourself down and be alert for people who need your smile, your kind words, or your helping hand. Make kindness a centerpiece of your dealings with others. They will be blessed, and you will be, too.

2 minutes A DAY

more stuff to think about

You will get untold flak for prioritizing God's revealed
and present will for your life over man's . . .
but, boy, is it worth it.

BETH MOORE

Don't stop the plough to kill a mouse. Do not hinder
important business for the discussion of a trifle.

C. H. SPURGEON

Our leisure, even our play, is a matter of serious concern.
There is no neutral ground in the universe:
every square inch, every split second,
is claimed by God and counterclaimed by Satan.

C. S. LEWIS

The Big Idea

First focus on God . . . and then everything else will come
into focus.

SELF-ESTEEM

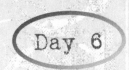

Take Time for Silence

My soul, wait silently for God alone,
For my expectation is from Him.
PSALM 62:5 NKJV

D o you take time each day for an extended period of silence? And during those precious moments, do you sincerely open your heart to your Creator? If so, you are wise and you are blessed.

The world can be a noisy place, a place filled to the brim with distractions, interruptions, and frustrations. And if you're not careful, the struggles and stresses of everyday living can rob you of the peace and the self-respect that should rightfully be yours because of your personal relationship with Christ. So take time each day to quietly commune with your Savior. When you do, those moments of silence will enable you to participate more fully in the only source of peace that endures: God's peace.

2 MINUTES A DAY

more stuff to think about

I always begin my prayers in silence,
for it is in the silence of the heart that God speaks.

MOTHER TERESA

If you, too, will learn to wait upon God, to get alone
with Him, and remain silent so that you can hear
His voice when He is ready to speak to you,
what a difference it will make in your life!

KAY ARTHUR

There are times when to speak is to violate the moment—
when silence represents the highest respect.
The world for such times is reverence.

MAX LUCADO

The Big Idea

Want to talk to God? Then don't make Him shout.
If you really want to hear from God, go to a quiet place
and listen. If you keep listening long enough and carefully
enough, He'll start talking.

SELF-ESTEEM

Be Careful How You Spend Your Time . . . and Your Life

There is an occasion for everything,
and a time for every activity under heaven.

ECCLESIASTES 3:1 HOLMAN CSB

I f you want to feel good about your life, then you'll need to do whatever it takes to feel good about the way that you spend your time. After all, how can you expect to build a healthy sense of self-worth if you're constantly goofing off— or doing things that you're not proud of?

Time is a nonrenewable gift from God, but sometimes, we treat our time here on earth as if it were not a gift at all: We may be tempted to invest far too much time in trivial pursuits and petty diversions. But our Father beckons each of us to a higher calling. God wants us to use our time wisely, to use it in accordance with His plan for our lives. And by the way, that's what we should want, too.

As you decide how you'll spend the time that's allotted to you here on earth, remember that each new day is a special treasure to be savored and celebrated. As a Christian, you have much to celebrate and much to do. It's up to you, and you alone, to honor God for the gift of time by using that gift wisely.

more stuff to think about

As we surrender the use of our time to the lordship of Christ,
He will lead us to use it in the most
productive way imaginable.

CHARLES STANLEY

Frustration is not the will of God. There is time to do
anything and everything that God wants us to do.

ELISABETH ELLIOT

To choose time is to save time.

FRANCIS BACON

The Big Idea

Feeling overwhelmed? Perhaps you're not doing a very good
job of setting priorities—or perhaps you're allowing other
people to set your priorities for you. In either case, perhaps
it's time for a change.

SELF-ESTEEM

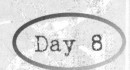
Learn How to Talk to Yourself Respectfully

*Give in to God, come to terms with him
and everything will turn out just fine.*
JOB 22:21 MSG

What are you telling yourself about yourself? When you look in the mirror, are you staring back at your biggest booster or your harshest critic? If you can learn to give yourself the benefit of the doubt—if you can learn how to have constructive conversations with the person you see in the mirror—then your self-respect will tend to take care of itself. But, if you're constantly berating yourself—if you're constantly telling yourself that you can't measure up—then you'll find that self-respect is always in short supply.

So, the next time you find yourself being critical of the person you see in the mirror, ask yourself if the criticism is really valid. If it is valid, make changes . . . if not, lighten up.

2 minutes A DAY

more stuff to think about

As you and I lay up for ourselves living,
lasting treasures in Heaven, we come to the awesome
conclusion that we ourselves are His treasure!

ANNE GRAHAM LOTZ

Your self worth is more important than your net worth.

ANONYMOUS

Living by grace inspires a growing consciousness
that I am what I am in the sight of Jesus and nothing more.
It is His approval that counts.

BRENNAN MANNING

The Big Idea

Pay careful attention to the way that you evaluate yourself.
And if you happen to be your own worst critic, it's time to
reevaluate the way that you've been evaluating (got that?)

SELF-ESTEEM

Don't Betray Your Conscience

So I strive always to keep my conscience
clear before God and man.
ACTS 24:16 NIV

Want to feel good about the person you see in the mirror? If so, here's a simple tip: don't betray your conscience.

It has been said that character is what we are when nobody is watching. How true. When we do things that we know aren't right, we try to hide them from our families and friends. But even then, God is watching.

Few things in life torment us more than a guilty conscience. And, few things in life provide more contentment than the knowledge that we are obeying the conscience that God has placed in our hearts.

If you sincerely want to create the best possible life for yourself and your loved ones, never forsake your conscience. And remember this: When you walk with God, your character will take care of itself . . . and you won't need to look over your shoulder to see who, besides God, is watching.

more stuff to think about

The convicting work of the Holy Spirit awakens,
disturbs, and judges.

FRANKLIN GRAHAM

Your conscience is your alarm system. It's your protection.

CHARLES STANLEY

It is neither safe nor prudent to do anything
against conscience.

MARTIN LUTHER

The Big Idea

That quiet little voice inside your head will guide you
down the right path if you listen carefully. Very often, your
conscience will actually tell you what God wants you to do.
So listen, learn, and behave accordingly. You'll feel better
about yourself when you do.

SELF-ESTEEM

Get Involved in a Church

*And I also say to you that you are Peter, and on this rock
I will build My church, and the forces of Hades will not
overpower it. I will give you the keys of the kingdom of
heaven, and whatever you bind on earth will have been
bound in heaven, and whatever you loose on earth
will have been loosed in heaven.*

MATTHEW 16:18-19 HOLMAN CSB

A good way to love yourself more is to worship with people who love and respect you. That's one reason (but certainly not the only reason) that you should be an active member of a supportive congregation.

Every believer—including you—needs to be part of a community of faith. Your association with fellow Christians should be uplifting, enlightening, encouraging, and consistent.

Are you an active member of your fellowship? Are you a builder of bridges inside the four walls of your church and outside it? Do you contribute your time and your talents to a close-knit band of hope-filled believers? Hopefully so. The fellowship of believers is intended to be a powerful tool for spreading God's Good News and uplifting His children. God intends for you to be a fully contributing member of that fellowship. Your intentions should be the same.

more stuff to think about

The church has no greater need today than to
fall in love with Jesus all over again.

VANCE HAVNER

Only participation in the full life of a local church
builds spiritual muscle.

RICK WARREN

In God's economy you will be hard-pressed to find
many examples of successful "Lone Rangers."

LUCI SWINDOLL

The Big Idea

If you become a fully participating member of an active
congregation, you'll become more excited about your faith,
your world, and yourself. So do yourself a favor: be an active
member of your fellowship.

SELF-ESTEEM

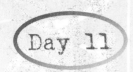

Find Friends Who Respect You

A friend loves at all times, and a brother is born for adversity.
PROVERBS 17:17 NIV

If you'd like to build a positive life and a positive self-image, hang out with friends who see the world—and you—in a positive light. When you do, you'll discover that good thoughts are contagious, and you can catch them from your friends.

As Christians, we have every reason to be optimistic about life. As John Calvin observed, "There is not one blade of grass, there is no color in this world that is not intended to make us rejoice." But, sometimes, rejoicing may be the last thing on our minds. Sometimes, we fall prey to worry, frustration, anxiety, or sheer exhaustion. And if we're not careful, we'll spread our pessimism to the people we love most. But God's Word instructs us to do otherwise.

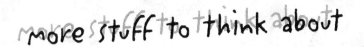
more stuff to think about

Inasmuch as anyone pushes you nearer to God,
he or she is your friend.

<small>BARBARA JOHNSON</small>

We long to find someone who has been where we've been,
who shares our fragile skies, who sees our sunsets
with the same shades of blue.

<small>BETH MOORE</small>

God has a plan for your friendships because He knows your
friends determine the quality and direction of your life.

<small>CHARLES STANLEY</small>

The Big Idea

Here's a simple, two-step way to build self-esteem:

1. Hang out with people who make you feel better about
yourself, not worse.

2. Hang out with people who encourage you to become a
better person, not worse.

SELF-ESTEEM

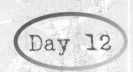

Date Wisely

Do not be unequally yoked together with unbelievers.
For what fellowship has righteousness with lawlessness?
And what communion has light with darkness?

2 CORINTHIANS 6:14 NKJV

Is God a part of your dating life? Hopefully so. If you sincerely want to know God, then you should date people who feel the same way.

If you're still searching for Mr. or Mrs. Right (while trying to avoid falling in love with Mr. or Mrs. Wrong), be patient, be prudent, and be picky. Look for someone whose values you respect, whose behavior you approve of, and whose faith you admire. Remember that appearances can be deceiving and tempting, so watch your step. And when it comes to the important task of building a lifetime relationship with the guy or girl of your dreams, pray about it!

When it comes to your dating life, God wants to give His approval—or not—but He won't give it until He's asked. So ask, listen, and decide accordingly.

more stuff to think about

The beauty of any relationship that bears fruit and life is that it is entered into of and by one's own choice.

DENNIS JERNIGAN

Line by line, moment by moment, special times are etched into our memories in the permanent ink of everlasting love in our relationships.

GLORIA GAITHER

It wasn't the apple, it was the pair.

ANONYMOUS

The Big Idea

Be choosy: Don't ever "settle" for second-class treatment—you deserve someone who values you as a person . . . and shows it.

SELF-ESTEEM

Day 13

Avoid Gossip

So rid yourselves of all wickedness,
all deceit, hypocrisy, envy, and all slander.
1 PETER 2:1 HOLMAN CSB

Face facts: gossip is the guilty little pleasure that tempts almost all of us from time to time. Why is it so tempting to gossip? Because when we put other people down, we experience a brief dose of self-righteousness as we look down our noses at the misdeeds of others. But there's a catch: In truth, we can never really build ourselves up by tearing other people down. So, the habit of gossip turns out to be a self-defeating waste of time.

It's no wonder that the Bible clearly teaches that gossip is wrong. Consider the simple advice found in Proverbs 16:28: "Gossip ruins friendships" (NCV). So do yourself a big favor: Don't spend precious time talking about other people. It's a waste of words, it's the wrong thing to do, and in the end, it will leave you with less self-respect, not more.

When you avoid the temptation to engage in gossip, you'll feel better about yourself—and other people will feel better about you, too. So don't do it.

2 minutes A DAY

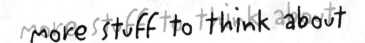

more stuff to think about

To belittle is to be little.

ANONYMOUS

I still believe we ought to talk about Jesus.
The old country doctor of my boyhood days always began
his examination by saying, "Let me see your tongue."
That's a good way to check a Christian: the tongue test.
Let's hear what he is talking about.

VANCE HAVNER

Would we want our hidden sins to be divulged?
Then we should be silent about the hidden sins of others.

ST. JEAN BAPTISTE DE LA SALLE

The Big Idea

When talking about other people, use this guideline: don't
say something behind someone's back that you wouldn't say
to that person directly.

SELF-ESTEEM

Avoid People Who Behave Foolishly

Do not be misled: "Bad company corrupts good character."
1 Corinthians 15:33 NIV

If you hang out with people who do dumb things, pretty soon, you'll probably find yourself doing dumb things, too. And that's bad . . . very bad. So, here's an ironclad rule for earning more self-respect and more rewards from life: If your peer group is headed in the wrong direction, find another peer group, and fast. Otherwise, before you know it, you'll be caught up in trouble that you didn't create and you don't deserve.

When you feel pressured to do things—or to say things—that lead you away from God, you're heading straight for trouble. So, don't do the "easy" thing or the "popular" thing. Do the right thing, and don't worry about winning any popularity contests.

2 minutes A DAY

more stuff to think about

Those who follow the crowd usually get lost in it.

RICK WARREN

We, as God's people, are not only to stay far away
from sin and sinners who would entice us,
but we are to be so like our God that we mourn over sin.

KAY ARTHUR

A person who deliberately and habitually sins is proving
that he does not know Christ and therefore
cannot be abiding in Him

WARREN WIERSBE

The Big Idea

A thoughtful Christian doesn't follow the crowd . . .
a thoughtful Christian follows Jesus (and he feels better
about himself when he does).

SELF-ESTEEM

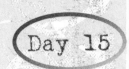

Have a Regular Appointment with God

Stay clear of silly stories that get dressed up as religion. Exercise daily in God—no spiritual flabbiness, please!

1 TIMOTHY 4:7 MSG

Want to feel better about yourself and your life? Then schedule a meeting with God every day. Daily life is a tapestry of habits, and no habit is more important to your spiritual health than the discipline of daily prayer and devotion to the Creator. When you begin each day with your head bowed and your heart lifted, you are reminded of God's love and God's laws.

Each day has 1,440 minutes—do you value your relationship with God enough to spend a few of those minutes with Him? He deserves that much of your time and more. But if you find that you're simply "too busy" for a daily chat with your Father in heaven, it's time to take a long, hard look at your priorities and your values.

If you've acquired the unfortunate habit of trying to "squeeze" God into the corners of your life, it's time to reshuffle the items on your to-do list by placing God first. God wants your undivided attention, not the leftovers of your day. So, if you haven't already done so, form the habit of spending quality time with your Creator. He deserves it . . . and so, for that matter, do you.

more stuff to think about

A person with no devotional life generally struggles
with faith and obedience.

CHARLES STANLEY

I suggest you discipline yourself to spend time daily
in a systematic reading of God's Word.
Make this "quiet time" a priority that nobody can change.

WARREN WIERSBE

I don't see how any Christian can survive,
let alone live life as more than a conqueror,
apart from a quiet time alone with God.

KAY ARTHUR

The Big Idea

Have you been too busy for a daily meeting with God?
If so, it's time to reorder your priorities. Make a promise
to yourself that you will begin each day with a morning
devotional. A regular time of quiet reflection and prayer will
allow to praise your Creator, to focus your thoughts, and
to seek God's guidance on matters great and small. Don't
miss this opportunity.

SELF-ESTEEM

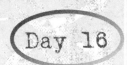

Steer Clear of Temptations

No temptation has seized you except what is common to man. And God is faithful; he will not let you be tempted beyond what you can bear. But when you are tempted, he will also provide a way out so that you can stand up under it.

1 Corinthians 10:13 NIV

Face facts: you live in a temptation-filled world. And if you cave in to those temptations, your sense of self-respect is headed south and fast.

The devil is hard at work in your neighborhood, and so are his helpers. Here in the 21st century, the bad guys are working around the clock to lead you astray. That's why you must remain vigilant.

In a letter to believers, Peter offers a stern warning: "Your adversary, the devil, prowls around like a roaring lion, seeking someone to devour" (I Peter 5:8 NASB). What was true in New Testament times is equally true in our own. Satan tempts his prey and then devours them (and it's up to you—and only you—to make sure that you're not one of the ones being devoured!)

As a believer who seeks a meaningful relationship with Jesus, you must beware because temptations are everywhere. Satan is determined to win; you must be equally determined that he does not.

more stuff to think about

We pursue righteousness when we flee the things that keep
us from following the Lord Jesus. These are the keys:
flee, follow, and fight.

FRANKLIN GRAHAM

Temptation is not a sin. Even Jesus was tempted.
The Lord Jesus gives you the strength needed
to resist temptation.

CORRIE TEN BOOM

Some temptations come to the industrious,
but all temptations attack the idle.

C. H. SPURGEON

The Big Idea

If life's inevitable temptations seem to be getting the best of
you, try praying more often, even if many of those prayers
are simply brief, "open-eyed" requests to your Father in
heaven.

SELF-ESTEEM

When Something Needs to Be Done, Do It

For the Kingdom of God is not just fancy talk;
it is living by God's power.
1 CORINTHIANS 4:20 NLT

When you know that something really needs to be done, you have a choice to make: You can either do the work that needs to be done, or you can put it off till later. If you get into the habit of doing things in a timely manner, you'll feel better about yourself (and you'll earn bigger rewards from life). But if you fall prey to the trap of procrastination, you'll pay a heavy price for your shortsightedness.

Are you one of those people who puts things off till the last minute? If so, it's time to change your ways. Your procrastination is probably the result of your shortsighted attempt to postpone (or avoid altogether) the discomfort that you associate with a particular activity. Get over it!

Whatever "it" is, do it now. When you do, you won't have to worry about "it" later—and that's very good news for you.

more stuff to think about

Let us not be content to wait and see what will happen,
but give us the determination to make
the right things happen.

PETER MARSHALL

Do noble things, do not dream them all day long.

CHARLES KINGSLEY

Action springs not from thought,
but from a readiness for responsibility.

DIETRICH BONHOEFFER

The Big Idea

When the time for action arrives, act. Procrastination is the
enemy of progress—and it can sabotage self-esteem—so
don't let self-imposed delays defeat you.

SELF-ESTEEM

Day 18

Don't Overestimate the Importance of Appearances

Man does not see what the LORD sees, for man sees what is visible, but the LORD sees the heart.
1 SAMUEL 15:7 HOLMAN CSB

The media wants you to believe that appearance is everything. According to the media, how you look is how you feel. But the media is mistaken: physical appearance usually has very little to do with self-respect. In fact, some of the most insecure people in the world are, surprisingly enough, those "beautiful" people who spend endless hours fussing over their physical appearance.

Have you made the mistake of linking your physical appearance to your self-respect? If so, it's time to start thinking differently. After all, the world sees you as you appear to be, but God sees you as you really are . . . He sees your heart, and He understands your intentions. That's what God cares about, and that's what you should care about, too.

more stuff to think about

Fashion is an enduring testimony to the fact that
we live quite consciously before the eyes of others.

JOHN ELDREDGE

Outside appearances, things like the clothes you wear
or the car you drive, are important to other people
but totally unimportant to God. Trust God.

MARIE T. FREEMAN

You will quickly be deceived if you look only to
the outward appearance of men, and you will often be
disappointed if you seek comfort and gain in them.

THOMAS À KEMPIS

The Big Idea

Appearances, appearances, appearances: don't be too
worried about what you look like on the outside—be more
concerned about the kind of person you are on the inside.
And while you're at it, don't judge other people by their
appearances, either.

SELF-ESTEEM

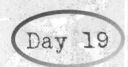

Find Worthwhile Things You Can Be Passionate About

Whatever you do, do all to the glory of God.
1 CORINTHIANS 10:31 NKJV

We all need to discover a purpose for our lives, a purpose that excites us and causes us to live each day with passion.

Anna Quindlen had this advice: "Consider the lilies of the field. Look at the fuzz on a baby's ear. Read in the backyard with the sun on your face. Learn to be happy. And think of life as a terminal illness, because, if you do, you will live it with joy and passion, as it ought to be lived."

If you have not yet discovered a passionate pursuit that blesses you and your world, don't allow yourself to become discouraged. Instead, keep searching and keep trusting that with God's help, you can—and will—find a meaningful way to serve your neighbors, your Creator, and yourself.

more stuff to think about

When we wholeheartedly commit ourselves to God,
there is nothing mediocre or run-of-the-mill about us.
To live for Christ is to be passionate about
our Lord and about our lives.

JIM GALLERY

Am I ignitable? God deliver me from the dread asbestos
of "other things." Saturate me with the oil of the Spirit
that I may be aflame.

JIM ELLIOT

The idea of always playing it safe, never venturing out of
our comfort zone, and refusing to broaden
the borders of our experience is stultifying.

MARILYN MEBERG

The Big Idea

Involve yourself in activities that you can support
wholeheartedly and enthusiastically. It's easier to celebrate
life—and it's easier to feel good about yourself—when
you're passionately involved in things you believe in.

SELF-ESTEEM

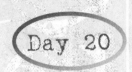

Avoid the Constant Critics

So encourage each other and give each other strength,
just as you are doing now.

1 THESSALONIANS 5:11 NCV

If you want to feel better about yourself, find friends who are willing to offer you a steady stream of encouragement. And while you're at it, steer clear of the ceaseless critics and the chronic fault-finders.

In the book of James, we are issued a clear warning: "Don't criticize one another, brothers" (4:11 Holman CSB). Undoubtedly, James understood the paralyzing power of chronic negativity, and so should you.

Negativity is highly contagious, and can be highly hazardous to your sense of self-worth. So, do yourself a major-league favor: find friends who make you feel better about yourself, not worse. Make no mistake: You deserve friends like that . . . and they deserve to have an encouraging friend like you.

2 minutes A DAY

more stuff to think about

It takes less sense to criticize than to do anything else.
There are a great many critics in the asylum.

SAM JONES

The scrutiny we give other people should be for ourselves.

OSWALD CHAMBERS

If I long to improve my brother, the first step toward
doing so is to improve myself.

CHRISTINA ROSSETTI

The Big Idea

Whether you realize it or not, you're a unique individual,
created by God, with special talents and one-of-a-kind
opportunities. Is that how you see yourself? If not, it's time to
correct your spiritual vision.

SELF-ESTEEM

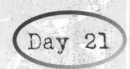

Stand Up for Your Beliefs

I know whom I have believed and am persuaded that He is able to guard what has been entrusted to me until that day.

2 TIMOTHY 1:12 HOLMAN CSB

In describing one's beliefs, actions are far better descriptors than words. Yet, far too many of us spend more energy talking about our beliefs than living by them—with predictable consequences.

Is your life a picture book of your creed? Are your actions congruent with your beliefs? Are you willing to practice the philosophy that you preach? If so, you'll most certainly feel better about yourself.

Today and every day, make certain that your actions are guided by God's Word and by the conscience that He has placed in your heart. Don't treat your faith as if it were separate from your everyday life. Weave your beliefs into the very fabric of your day. When you do, God will honor your good works, and your good works will honor God.

more stuff to think about

I do not seek to understand that I may believe,
but I believe in order to understand.

ST. AUGUSTINE

Belief is not the result of an intellectual act;
it is the result of an act of my will whereby
I deliberately commit myself.

OSWALD CHAMBERS

You may as well quit reading and hearing
the Word of God and give it to the devil if you do not desire
to live according to it.

MARTIN LUTHER

The Big Idea

When you stand up for your beliefs—and when you follow
your conscience—you'll feel better about yourself. When you
don't, you won't.

SELF-ESTEEM

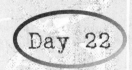

Know When Not to Quit

*Let us not become weary in doing good, for at the proper
time we will reap a harvest if we do not give up.*

GALATIANS 6:9 NIV

The occasional disappointments and failures of life are
inevitable. Such setbacks are simply the price that we
must pay for our willingness to take risks as we follow
our dreams. But even when we encounter setbacks, we must
never lose faith.

The reassuring words of Hebrews 10:36 serve as a
comforting reminder that perseverance indeed pays: "You
have need of endurance, so that when you have done the
will of God, you may receive what was promised" (NASB).

Are you willing to trust God's Word? And are you
willing to keep "fighting the good fight," even when you've
experienced unexpected difficulties? If so, you may soon
be surprised at the creative ways that God finds to help
determined people like you . . . people who possess the
wisdom and the courage to persevere.

2 minutes A DAY

more stuff to think about

Failure is one of life's most powerful teachers.
How we handle our failures determines whether
we're going to simply "get by" in life or "press on."

BETH MOORE

Every achievement worth remembering is stained
with the blood of diligence and scarred by
the wounds of disappointment.

CHARLES SWINDOLL

Keep adding, keep walking, keep advancing; do not stop,
do not turn back, do not turn from the straight road.

ST. AUGUSTINE

The Big Idea

If things don't work out at first, don't quit. If you never try,
you'll never know how good you can be.

SELF-ESTEEM

Keep Learning, Keep Growing

So let us stop going over the basics of Christianity again and again. Let us go on instead and become mature in our understanding.

HEBREWS 6:1 NLT

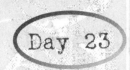

Another way to take care of yourself is to keep growing spiritually. The journey toward spiritual maturity lasts a lifetime. As Christians, we can and should continue to grow in the love and the knowledge of our Savior as long as we live. Norman Vincent Peale had the following advice for believers of all ages: "Ask the God who made you to keep remaking you." That advice, of course, is perfectly sound, but often ignored.

When we cease to grow, either emotionally or spiritually, we do ourselves a profound disservice. But, if we study God's Word, if we obey His commandments, and if we live in the center of His will, we will not be "stagnant" believers; we will, instead, be growing Christians . . . and that's exactly what God wants for our lives.

more stuff to think about

God's goal is that we move toward maturity—
all our past failures and faults notwithstanding.

CHARLES SWINDOLL

You are free to choose, but the choices you make today will
determine what you will have, what you will be,
and what you will do in the tomorrow of your life.

ZIG ZIGLAR

Today is yesterday's pupil.

THOMAS FULLER

The Big Idea

If you are determined to keep growing spiritually and
intellectually, you'll feel better about yourself. So what are
you waiting for?

SELF-ESTEEM

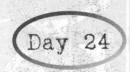

Avoid the Wrong Kind of Peer Pressure

Whoever walks with the wise will become wise;
whoever walks with fools will suffer harm.

PROVERBS 13:20 NLT

Peer pressure can be good or bad, depending upon who your peers are and how they behave. If your friends encourage you to follow God's will and to obey His commandments, then you'll experience positive peer pressure, and that's a good thing. But, if your friends encourage you to do foolish things, then you're facing a different kind of peer pressure . . . and you'd better beware.

Do you want to feel good about yourself and your life? If so, here's a simple, proven strategy: Go out and find friends who, by their words and their actions, will help you build the kind of life that's worth feeling good about.

more stuff to think about

Nothing can be more dangerous than keeping wicked companions. They communicate the infection of their vices to all who associate with them.

St. Jean Baptiste de la Salle

Choose the opposition of the whole world rather than offend Jesus.

Thomas à Kempis

You'll probably end up behaving like your friends behave . . . and if that's a scary thought, it's time to make a new set of friends.

Criswell Freeman

The Big Idea

If you're hanging out with friends who behave badly, you're heading straight for trouble. To avoid negative consequences, pick friends who avoid negative behaviors.

SELF-ESTEEM

Be a Kind Person

Finally, all of you be of one mind, having compassion for one another; love as brothers, be tenderhearted, be courteous.

1 PETER 3:8 NKJV

It's a fact: when we do kind things, we feel better about ourselves. The words of Matthew 7:12 remind us that, as believers in Christ, we are commanded to treat others as we wish to be treated. This commandment is, indeed, the Golden Rule for Christians of every generation.

Kindness is a choice. Sometimes, when we feel happy or successful, we find it easy to be kind. Other times, when we are discouraged or tired, we can scarcely summon the energy to utter a single kind word. But, God's commandment is clear: we must observe the Golden Rule "in everything." God intends that we make the conscious choice to treat others with kindness and respect, no matter our circumstances, no matter our emotions. Kindness, therefore, is a choice that we, as Christians, must make many times each day.

When we weave the thread of kindness into the very fabric of our lives, we give a priceless gift to others, and we give glory to the One who gave His life for us. As believers, we must do no less.

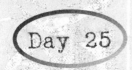
2 minutes A DAY

more stuff to think about

Do all the good you can. By all the means you can.
In all the ways you can. In all the places you can.
At all the times you can. To all the people you can.
As long as ever you can.

JOHN WESLEY

If we have the true love of God in our hearts,
we will show it in our lives. We will not have to go up
and down the earth proclaiming it.
We will show it in everything we say or do.

D. L. MOODY

One of the greatest things a man can do for his
heavenly Father is to be kind to some of his other children.

HENRY DRUMMOND

The Big Idea

When you respect other people, they're more likely to
respect you . . . so everybody feels better about themselves.

SELF-ESTEEM

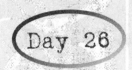

Always Tell the Truth

*Better to be poor and honest than a rich person
no one can trust.*
PROVERBS 19:1 MSG

It has been said on many occasions and in many ways that honesty is the best policy. But it's far more important to note that honesty is God's policy. And it's also worth noting that you'll respect yourself more when you make a rock-solid commitment to be a person of integrity.

Sometimes, honesty is difficult; sometimes, honesty is painful; sometimes, honesty makes us feel uncomfortable. Despite these temporary feelings of discomfort, we must make honesty the hallmark of all our relationships; otherwise, we invite needless suffering into our own lives and into the lives of those we love.

Sometime soon, perhaps even today, you will be tempted to bend the truth or perhaps even to break it. Resist that temptation. Truth is God's way…and it must be your way, too.

2 minutes a day

more stuff to think about

Honest men fear neither the light nor the dark.

THOMAS FULLER

Those who, to please their listeners, avoid giving a forthright
declaration of the will of God become slaves of those
they would please and abandon the service of God.

ST. BASIL THE GREAT

God doesn't expect you to be perfect,
but he does insist on complete honesty.

RICK WARREN

The Big Idea

Beware of "white" lies. Sometimes, you may be tempted
to "shade" the truth. Unfortunately, little white lies have a
tendency to turn black . . . and they grow. The best strategy
is to avoid untruths of all sizes and colors. And remember
this: you'll feel better about yourself when you know that
you've been honest with yourself and with others.

SELF-ESTEEM

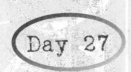

Remember: You Don't Have to Be Perfect

Those who wait for perfect weather will never plant seeds;
those who look at every cloud will never harvest crops . . . .
Plant early in the morning, and work until evening,
because you don't know if this or that will succeed.
They might both do well.

ECCLESIASTES 11:4,6 NCV

Expectations, expectations, expectations! The media delivers an endless stream of messages that tell you how to look, how to behave, and how to dress. The media's expectations are impossible to meet—God's are not. God doesn't expect perfection . . . and neither should you.

If you find yourself bound up by the chains of perfectionism, it's time to ask yourself who you're trying to impress, and why. If you're trying to impress other people, it's time to reconsider your priorities. Your first responsibility is to the heavenly Father who created you and to His Son who saved you. Then, you bear a powerful responsibility to your family. But, when it comes to meeting society's unrealistic expectations, forget it!

Remember that when you accepted Christ as your Savior, God accepted you for all eternity. Now, it's your turn to accept yourself and your loved ones. When you do, you'll feel a tremendous weight being lifted from your shoulders. After all, pleasing God is simply a matter of obeying His commandments and accepting His Son. But as for pleasing everybody else? That's impossible!

more stuff to think about

The happiest people in the world are not those who have no problems, but the people who have learned to live with those things that are less than perfect.

JAMES DOBSON

What makes a Christian a Christian is not perfection but forgiveness.

MAX LUCADO

The Big Idea

Don't be too hard on yourself: you don't have to be perfect to be wonderful.

SELF-ESTEEM

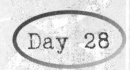

Day 28

Treat Addictive Substances Like Poison

*Be sober! Be on the alert! Your adversary
the Devil is prowling around like a roaring lion,
looking for anyone he can devour.*

1 PETER 5:8 HOLMAN CSB

If you'd like a perfect formula for low (or no) self-respect, here it is: get addicted to something that destroys your health or your sanity. If (God forbid) you allow yourself to become addicted, you're steering straight for a boatload of negative consequences, not to mention a big bad dose of negative self-esteem.

Unless you're living on a deserted island, you know people who are full-blown addicts—probably lots of people. If you, or someone you love, is suffering from the blight of addiction, remember this: Help is available. Plenty of people have experienced addiction and lived to tell about it . . . so don't give up hope.

And if you're one of those fortunate people who hasn't started experimenting with addictive substances, congratulations! You have just spared yourself a lifetime of headaches and heartaches.

more stuff to think about

One reason I'm a teetotaler is that I got so disgusted being mistreated due to a man's drinking to excess that I never have wanted to run the risk of mistreating my own family by drinking.

JERRY CLOWER

A man may not be responsible for his last drink, but he certainly was for the first.

BILLY GRAHAM

When I feel like circumstances are spiraling downward in my life, God taught me that whether I'm right side up or upside down, I need to turn those circumstances over to Him. He is the only one who can bring balance into my life.

CAROLE LEWIS

The Big Idea

Warning: Addiction and self-esteem can't live for long in the same body.

SELF-ESTEEM

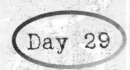

Treat Your Body with Respect

*Don't you know that you are God's temple
and that God's Spirit lives in you?*

1 CORINTHIANS 3:16 NCV

One of the quickest ways to destroy your self-esteem is to start treating your body with disrespect.

How do you treat your body? Do you treat it with the reverence and respect it deserves, or do you take it more or less for granted? Well, the Bible has clear instructions about the way you should take care of the miraculous body that God has given you.

God's Word teaches us that our bodies are "temples" which belong to God (1 Corinthians 6:19-20). We are commanded (not encouraged, not advised—we are commanded!) to treat our bodies with respect and honor. We do so by making wise choices and by making those choices consistently over an extended period of time.

Do you sincerely seek to improve the overall quality of your life and your health? Then promise yourself—and God—that you'll begin making the kind of wise choices that will lead to a longer, healthier, happier life. The responsibility for those choices is yours. And so are the rewards.

more stuff to think about

God wants you to give Him your body.
Some people do foolish things with their bodies.
God wants your body as a holy sacrifice.

WARREN WIERSBE

People are funny. When they are young, they will spend their
health to get wealth. Later, they will gladly pay
all they have trying to get their health back.

JOHN MAXWELL

Our body is a portable sanctuary through which
we are daily experiencing the presence of God.

RICHARD FOSTER

The Big Idea

God has given you a marvelous gift: your body. Taking
care of that body is your responsibility. Don't dodge that
responsibility! Give your body the respect it deserves.

SELF-ESTEEM

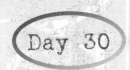

Establish a Growing Relationship with Jesus

But whoever keeps His word, truly in him the love of God is perfected. This is how we know we are in Him: the one who says he remains in Him should walk just as He walked.

1 JOHN 2:5-6 HOLMAN CSB

When you establish a dynamic relationship with Jesus, you'll feel better about yourself, your future, and your world. Jesus walks with you. Are you walking with Him? Hopefully, you will choose to walk with Him today and every day of your life.

Jesus has called upon believers of every generation (and that includes you) to follow in His footsteps. And God's Word promises that when you follow in Christ's footsteps, you will learn how to live freely and lightly (Matthew 11:28-30).

Are you dealing with issues of self-confidence, self-esteem, or self-respect? Talk to God about your concerns. He's always available. Are you worried about the future? Be courageous and call upon God. He will protect you. Are you confused? Listen to the quiet voice of your Heavenly Father. He is not a God of confusion. Talk with God; listen to Him; follow His commandments . . . and walk with His Son—starting now, and ending never.

more stuff to think about

As a child of God, rest in the knowledge that your
Savior precedes you, and He will walk with you
through each experience of your life.

HENRY BLACKABY

Only by walking with God can we hope to find
the path that leads to life.

JOHN ELDREDGE

Our responsibility is to feed from Him, to stay close to Him,
to follow Him—because sheep easily go astray—so that we
eternally experience the protection and companionship of
our Great Shepherd the Lord Jesus Christ.

FRANKLIN GRAHAM

The Big Idea

If you want to be a disciple of Christ . . . follow in His
footsteps, obey His commandments, and share His never-
ending love. When you do, you'll feel better about your
world, your faith, your future, and yourself.

SELF-ESTEEM

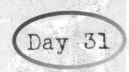
Be an Optimist

For God has not given us a spirit of fear,
but of power and of love and of a sound mind.
2 TIMOTHY 1:7 NLT

There are few sadder sights on earth than the sight of a girl or guy who has lost hope. In difficult times, hope can be elusive, but those who place their faith in God's promises need never lose it. After all, God is good; His love endures; He has promised His children the gift of eternal life. And, God keeps His promises.

Today, make this promise to yourself and keep it: vow to be a hope-filled Christian. Think optimistically about your life, your education, your family, and your future. Trust your hopes, not your fears. Take time to celebrate God's glorious creation. And then, when you've filled your heart with hope, share your optimism with others. They'll be better for it, and so will you.

2 minutes A DAY

more stuff to think about

Keep your feet on the ground, but let your heart soar
as high as it will. Refuse to be average or to surrender
to the chill of your spiritual environment.

A. W. Tozer

Developing a positive attitude means working continually
to find what is uplifting and encouraging.

Barbara Johnson

Stop thinking wishfully and start living hopefully.

Emilie Barnes

The Big Idea

Be a realistic optimist. You should strive to think realistically
about the future, but you should never confuse realism
with pessimism. Your attitude toward the future will help
create your future, so you might as well put the self-fulfilling
prophecy to work for you by being both a realist and an
optimist. And remember that life is far too short to be a
pessimist.

SELF-ESTEEM

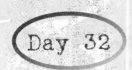
Don't Become Your Own Worst Critic

Happy is he who does not condemn himself . . . .
ROMANS 14:22 NASB

Are you your own worst critic? If so, it's time to become a little more understanding of the unique and wonderful person you see whenever you look into the mirror.

Millions of words have been written about various ways to improve self-image and increase self-esteem. Yet, maintaining a healthy self-image is, to a surprising extent, a matter of doing three things: 1. behaving yourself 2. thinking healthy thoughts 3. finding a purpose for your life that pleases your Creator and yourself.

The Bible affirms the importance of self-acceptance by teaching Christians to love others as they love themselves (Matthew 22:37-40). God accepts us just as we are. And, if He accepts us—faults and all—then who are we to believe otherwise?

more stuff to think about

Being loved by Him whose opinion matters most gives us
the security to risk loving, too—even loving ourselves.

GLORIA GAITHER

Your core identity—and particularly your perception of
it—plays a vital role in determining how you carry yourself in
daily life, how much joy you experience, how you treat other
people, and how you respond to God.

JOSH MCDOWELL

The Big Idea

If God thinks you're beautiful, why do you feel so average?
Perhaps it's because you're trying to live up to impossible
standards! If you listen to the messages that spew out of the
media, you'll convince yourself that you can never be pretty
enough, thin enough, smart enough, or rich enough. But
God doesn't care about stuff like that, and neither should
you. God loves you just like you are . . . and now, it's your
turn to do the same thing.

SELF-ESTEEM

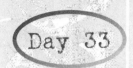

Forgive People Sooner Rather Than Later

You have heard that it was said, "Love your neighbor and hate your enemies." But I say to you, love your enemies. Pray for those who hurt you.

MATTHEW 5:43-44 NCV

It's hard to feel good about yourself while you're carrying around a heart full of bitterness. That's one reason (but not the only reason) that you should be quick to forgive everybody.

If there exists even one person whom you have not forgiven (and that includes yourself), follow God's commandment and His will for your life: forgive that person today. And remember that bitterness, anger, and regret are not part of God's plan for your life. Forgiveness is.

If you sincerely wish to forgive someone, pray for that person. And then pray for yourself by asking God to heal your heart. Don't expect forgiveness to be easy or quick, but rest assured: with God as your partner, you can forgive . . . and you will.

more stuff to think about

God has been very gracious to me, for I never dwell
upon anything wrong which a person has done to me,
as to remember it afterwards. If I do remember it,
I always see some other virtue in the person.

ST. TERESA OF AVILA

Mercy imitates God and disappoints Satan.

ST. JOHN CHRYSOSTOM

Our Lord worked with people as they were, and He was
patient—not tolerant of sin, but compassionate.

VANCE HAVNER

The Big Idea

When other people have made a mistake . . . it's a mistake
not to forgive them.

SELF-ESTEEM

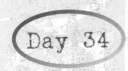

Learn How to Deal with Rejection

*Wherever they do not welcome you, when you leave
that town, shake off the dust from your feet
as a testimony against them.*

LUKE 9:5 HOLMAN CSB

I f you're like most people, you're sensitive to rejection. But you should be aware that the fear of rejection can be a major roadblock on the path to a purposeful life. Why? Because the more fearful you are of displeasing others, the more likely you are to make decisions that are not in your best interest.

When you try to please everybody in sight, you create for yourself a task that is unrealistic, unsatisfying, and unworthy of your efforts. A far better strategy, of course, is to concentrate, first and foremost, on pleasing God. But sometimes, that's easier said than done, especially if you focus too intently on being a "people pleaser."

So, focus your thoughts and energies on pleasing your Creator first and always. And when it comes to the world and all its inhabitants, don't worry too much about the folks you can't please. Focus, instead, on doing the right thing—and leave the rest up to God.

more stuff to think about

What may seem defeat to us may be victory to him.

C. H. SPURGEON

The enemy of our souls loves to taunt us with past failures,
wrongs, disappointments, disasters, and calamities.
And if we let him continue doing this, our life becomes
a long and dark tunnel, with very little light at the end.

CHARLES SWINDOLL

When you taste a measure of being able to love and enjoy
the people in your life, without having to have any particular
response from them, you are tasting bliss.

PAULA RINEHART

The Big Idea

If you're feeling discouraged, try to redirect your thoughts
away from the troubles that plague you—focus, instead,
upon the opportunities that surround you.

SELF-ESTEEM

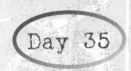

Pray Early and Often

Be cheerful no matter what; pray all the time; thank God no matter what happens. This is the way God wants you who belong to Christ Jesus to live.

1 THESSALONIANS 5:16-18 MSG

Perhaps, because of your demanding schedule, you've neglected to pay sufficient attention to a particularly important part of your life: the spiritual part. If so, today is the day to change, and one way to make that change is simply to spend a little more time talking with God.

God is trying to get His message through to you. Are you listening?

Perhaps, on occasion, you may find yourself overwhelmed by the press of everyday life. Perhaps you may forget to slow yourself down long enough to talk with God. Instead of turning your thoughts and prayers to Him, you may rely upon your own resources. Instead of asking God for guidance, you may depend only upon your own limited wisdom. A far better course of action is this: simply stop what you're doing long enough to open your heart to God; then listen carefully for His directions.

In all things great and small, seek God's wisdom and His grace. He hears your prayers, and He will answer. All you must do is ask.

more stuff to think about

Four things let us ever keep in mind:
God hears prayer, God heeds prayer, God answers prayer,
and God delivers by prayer.

E. M. BOUNDS

We must pray literally without ceasing, in every occurrence
and employment of our lives. You know I mean that prayer
of the heart which is independent of place or situation, or
which is, rather, a habit of lifting up the heart to God,
as in a constant communication with Him.

ELIZABETH ANN SETON

Do nothing at all unless you begin with prayer.

EPHRAEM THE SYRIAN

The Big Idea

Of course you should pray at mealtime and bedtime, but
that's just the beginning. You can offer lots of prayers to God
all day long . . . and you should!

SELF-ESTEEM

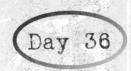

Don't Fall Prey to the Media Hype

For those whose lives are according to the flesh think about the things of the flesh, but those whose lives are according to the Spirit, about the things of the Spirit.

ROMANS 8:5 HOLMAN CSB

Sometimes it's hard to feel satisfied with yourself, especially if you pay much attention to all those messages that media keeps pumping out. Those messages, which seem to pop up just about everywhere, try to tell you how you should look, how you should behave, and what you should buy.

The media isn't interested in making you feel good about yourself—far from it. The media is interested in selling you stuff. And one of the best ways that marketers can find to sell you things is by making you feel dissatisfied with yourself and with your situation. That's why the folks from the media are working 24/7 to rearrange your priorities.

And that's why it's important for you to make sure that they don't.

more stuff to think about

Because the world is deceptive, it is dangerous.
The world can even deceive God's own people
and lead them into trouble.

WARREN WIERSBE

The problem is that the culture seeps into the church,
bringing with it a religion without commitment;
spirituality without content; aspiration and talk and longing,
fulfillment and needs, but not much concern about God.

EUGENE PETERSON

Why is love of gold more potent than love of souls?

LOTTIE MOON

The Big Idea

If you dwell on the world's message, you're setting yourself
up for disaster. If you dwell on God's message, you're setting
yourself up for victory.

SELF-ESTEEM

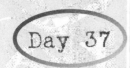

Keep Your Fears in Perspective

They won't be afraid of bad news; their hearts are steady because they trust the Lord.

PSALM 112:7 NCV

His adoring fans called him the "Sultan of Swat." He was Babe Ruth, the baseball player who set records for home runs and strikeouts. Babe's philosophy was simple. He said, "Never let the fear of striking out get in your way." That's smart advice on the diamond or off.

Of course it's never wise to take foolish risks (so buckle up, slow down, and don't do anything silly). But when it comes to the game of life, you should not let the fear of failure keep you from taking your swings.

Today, ask God for the courage to step beyond the boundaries of your self-doubts. Ask Him to guide you to a place where you can realize your full potential—a place where you are freed from the fear of failure. Ask Him to do His part, and promise Him that you will do your part. Don't ask Him to lead you to a "safe" place; ask Him to lead you to the "right" place . . . and remember: those two places are seldom the same.

2 minutes A DAY

more stuff to think about

Earthly fears are no fears at all.
Answer the big question of eternity,
and the little questions of life fall into perspective.

MAX LUCADO

I have found the perfect antidote for fear.
Whenever it sticks up its ugly face, I clobber it with prayer.

DALE EVANS ROGERS

When once we are assured that God is good,
then there can be nothing left to fear.

HANNAH WHITALL SMITH

The Big Idea

Everybody faces obstacles. Don't overestimate the size of
yours.

SELF-ESTEEM

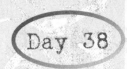

Have an Eternal Perspective

Dear friends, don't let this one thing escape you:
with the Lord one day is like 1,000 years,
and 1,000 years like one day.

2 PETER 3:8 HOLMAN CSB

God's plans for you, big plans, extend throughout all eternity.

Christ sacrificed His life on the cross so that you might have eternal life. This gift, freely given by God's only begotten Son, is the priceless possession of everyone who accepts Him as Lord and Savior—when you welcome Jesus into your heart, you have nothing to fear today, tomorrow, or ever.

So, as you struggle with the inevitable hardships and occasional disappointments of everyday life, remember that God has invited you to accept His abundance not only for today but also for all time. So, keep things in perspective. Although you will inevitably encounter occasional defeats in this world, you'll have all eternity to celebrate the ultimate victory in the next.

more stuff to think about

Let us see the victorious Jesus, the conqueror of the tomb,
the one who defied death. And let us be reminded that we,
too, will be granted the same victory.

MAX LUCADO

For a small reward a man will hurry away to a long journey
while for eternal life many will hardly take a step.

THOMAS À KEMPIS

Live near to God, and all things will appear little
to you in comparison with eternal realities.

ROBERT MURRAY MCCHEYNE

The Big Idea

People love talking about religion, and everybody has their
own opinions, but ultimately only one opinion counts . . .
God's. Talk to your friends about God's promise of eternal
life—what that promise means to you and what it should
mean to them.

SELF-ESTEEM

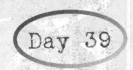

Don't Be Envious

*We can't afford to waste a minute, must not squander
these precious daylight hours in frivolity and indulgence,
in sleeping around and dissipation, in bickering and
grabbing everything in sight. Get out of bed and get dressed!
Don't loiter and linger, waiting until the very last minute.
Dress yourselves in Christ, and be up and about!*

ROMANS 13:13-14 MSG

Because we are frail, imperfect human beings, we are
sometimes envious of others. But God's Word warns
us that envy is sin. Thus, we must guard ourselves
against the natural tendency to feel resentment and jealousy
when other people experience good fortune.

As believers, we have absolutely no reason to be
envious of any people on earth. After all, as Christians we
are already recipients of the greatest gift in all creation:
God's grace. We have been promised the gift of eternal life
through God's only begotten Son, and we must count that
gift as our most precious possession.

Rather than succumbing to the sin of envy, we should
focus on the marvelous things that God has done for
us—starting with Christ's sacrifice. And we must refrain from
preoccupying ourselves with the blessings that God has
chosen to give others.

So, here's a surefire formula for a happier, healthier life: Count your own blessings and let your neighbors count theirs. It's the godly way to live.

more stuff to think about

How can you possess the miseries of envy when you possess in Christ the best of all portions?

C. H. SPURGEON

Comparison is the root of all feelings of inferiority.

JAMES DOBSON

Contentment comes when we develop an attitude of gratitude for the important things we do have in our lives that we tend to take for granted if we have our eyes staring longingly at our neighbor's stuff.

DAVE RAMSEY

The Big Idea

Feelings of envy rob you of happiness and peace. Why rob yourself?

SELF-ESTEEM

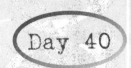
Look for Fulfillment in the Right Places

I am the Gate. Anyone who goes through me will be cared for—will freely go in and out, and find pasture. A thief is only there to steal and kill and destroy. I came so they can have real and eternal life, more and better life than they ever dreamed of. "I am the Good Shepherd. The Good Shepherd puts the sheep before himself, sacrifices himself if necessary."

JOHN 10:9-11 MSG

Where can we find contentment? Is it a result of wealth or power or beauty or fame? Hardly. Genuine contentment is a gift from God to those who trust Him and follow His commandments.

Our modern world seems preoccupied with the search for happiness. We are bombarded with messages telling us that happiness depends upon the acquisition of material possessions. These messages are false. Enduring peace is not the result of our acquisitions; it is a spiritual gift from God to those who obey Him and accept His will.

If we don't find contentment in God, we will never find it anywhere else. But, if we seek Him and obey Him, we will be blessed with an inner peace that is beyond human understanding. When God dwells at the center of our lives, peace and contentment will belong to us just as surely as we belong to God.

more stuff to think about

We will never be happy until we make God the source
of our fulfillment and the answer to our longings.

STORMIE OMARTIAN

If you want purpose and meaning and satisfaction and
fulfillment and peace and hope and joy and abundant life
that lasts forever, look to Jesus.

ANNE GRAHAM LOTZ

God's riches are beyond anything we could ask
or even dare to imagine! If my life gets gooey and stale,
I have no excuse.

BARBARA JOHNSON

The Big Idea

If you're not contented, try focusing less on "stuff" and more
on God.

SELF-ESTEEM

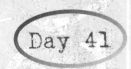

Have the Courage
to Trust God

*Trust the Lord with all your heart, and don't depend
on your own understanding. Remember the Lord
in all you do, and he will give you success.*

PROVERBS 3:5-6 NCV

As the journey through this life unfolds day by day, we are confronted with situations that we simply don't understand. But God does. And He has a reason for everything that He does. Furthermore, God doesn't explain Himself in ways that we, as mortals with limited insight and clouded vision, can comprehend. So, instead of understanding every aspect of God's unfolding plan for our lives and our universe, we must be satisfied to trust Him completely. We cannot know God's motivations, nor can we understand His actions. We can, however, trust Him, and we must.

more stuff to think about

Down through the centuries, in times of trouble and trial,
God has brought courage to the hearts of those who love
Him. The Bible is filled with assurances of God's help
and comfort in every kind of trouble which might cause
fears to arise in the human heart. You can look ahead
with promise, hope, and joy.

BILLY GRAHAM

Conditions are always changing; therefore, I must not be
dependent upon conditions. What matters supremely is
my soul and my relationship to God.

CORRIE TEN BOOM

True faith is man's weakness leaning on God's strength.

D. L. MOODY

The Big Idea

If you'd like infinite protection, there's only one place you
can receive it: from an infinite God. So remember: when you
live in the center of God's will, you will also be living in the
center of God's protection.

SELF-ESTEEM

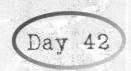

Get to Know God's Book

As newborn babies want milk, you should want the pure and simple teaching. By it you can grow up and be saved.

1 PETER 2:2 NCV

When it comes to your faith, God doesn't intend for you to stand still. He wants you to keep moving and growing. In fact, God's plan for you includes a lifetime of prayer, praise, and spiritual growth.

As a Christian, you should continue to grow in the love and the knowledge of your Savior as long as you live. How? By studying God's Word every day, by obeying His commandments, and by allowing His Son to reign over your heart, that's how.

Are you continually seeking to become a more mature believer? Hopefully so, because that's exactly what you owe to yourself and to God . . . but not necessarily in that order.

2 minutes A DAY

more stuff to think about

There is no way to draw closer to God unless you are in the
Word of God every day. It's your compass. Your guide.
You can't get where you need to go without it.

STORMIE OMARTIAN

When you meet with God, open the Bible.
Don't rely on your memory; rely on those printed pages.

CHARLES SWINDOLL

Voltaire expected that within fifty years of his lifetime there
would not be one Bible in the world. Today, his house is
a distribution center for Bibles in many languages.

CORRIE TEN BOOM

The Big Idea

God wrote a Book that He wants you to read. And if you
think you're too busy to read it, He wants you to think again.

SELF-ESTEEM

Face Up to Your Responsibilities

We want each of you to go on with the same hard work
all your lives so you will surely get what you hope for.
We do not want you to become lazy. Be like those
who through faith and patience will receive what
God has promised.

HEBREWS 6:11–12 NCV

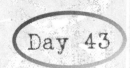

These words from the sixth chapter of Hebrews remind us that as Christians we must labor diligently, patiently, and faithfully. Do you want to be a worthy example for your family and friends? And would you like to give a big-time boost to your sense of self-worth? If so, you must preach the gospel of responsible behavior, not only with your words, but also by your actions.

Do you want to feel better about yourself, your future, and your world? Of course you do. And of course you should be willing to work diligently for the rewards you seek.

End of lecture.

2 MINUTES A DAY

more stuff to think about

Every time you refuse to face up to life and its problems,
you weaken your character.

E. STANLEY JONES

Do not pray for easy lives. Pray to be stronger men!
Do not pray for tasks equal to your powers.
Pray for powers equal to your tasks.

PHILLIPS BROOKS

Help yourself and God will help you.

ST. JOAN OF ARC

The Big Idea

When you accept responsibilities and fulfill them, you'll feel
better about yourself. When you avoid your obligations, you
won't. Act accordingly.

SELF-ESTEEM

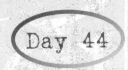

Be Thankful for God's Gifts

Thanks be to God for his indescribable gift!
2 CORINTHIANS 9:15 NIV

How do we thank God for the gifts He has given us? By using those gifts for the glory of His kingdom. God has given you talents and opportunities that are uniquely yours. Are you willing to use your gifts in the way that God intends? And are you willing to summon the discipline that is required to develop your talents and to hone your skills? That's precisely what God wants you to do, and that's precisely what you should desire for yourself.

As you seek to expand your talents, you will undoubtedly encounter stumbling blocks along the way, such as the fear of rejection or the fear of failure. When you do, don't stumble! Just continue to refine your skills and offer your services to God. And when the time is right, He will use you—but it's up to you to be thoroughly prepared when He does.

more stuff to think about

What we are is God's gift to us.
What we become is our gift to God.

ANONYMOUS

The ability to rejoice in any situation is a sign
of spiritual maturity.

BILLY GRAHAM

Go outside, to the fields, enjoy nature and the sunshine,
go out and try to recapture happiness in yourself
and in God. Think of all the beauty that's still left in
and around you and be happy!

ANNE FRANK

The Big Idea

God gives each of us more blessings than we can count.
Those blessings include life, family, freedom, friends, talents,
and possessions, just for starters. Winners recognize the size
and scope of God's blessings—and real winners (like you)
spend plenty of time thanking Him.

SELF-ESTEEM

Day 45

Be Generous

God loves the person who gives cheerfully.
2 Corinthians 9:7 NLT

Are you a cheerful giver? If you intend to obey God's commandments, you must be. When you give, God looks not only at the quality of your gift, but also at the condition of your heart. If you give generously, joyfully, and without complaint, you'll feel good about yourself because you'll know that you're obeying God's Word. But, if you make your gifts grudgingly, or if the motivation for your gift is selfish, you'll be doing a disservice to yourself and your Creator.

Today, take God's commandments to heart and make this pledge: Be a cheerful, generous, courageous giver. The world needs your help, and you need the spiritual rewards that will be yours when you give faithfully, prayerfully, and cheerfully.

more stuff to think about

A happy spirit takes the grind out of giving.
The grease of gusto frees the gears of generosity.

CHARLES SWINDOLL

The rich man is not one who possesses much,
but one who gives much.

ST. JOHN CHRYSOSTOM

Giving to God and, in His name, to others,
is not something that we do; it is the result of what we are.

WARREN WIERSBE

The Big Idea

Want to admire the person you see in the mirror? Try being a little more generous. The more generous you are, the better you'll feel about yourself.

SELF-ESTEEM

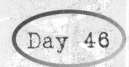

Be Wise Enough to Be Moderate

Watch out! Don't let me find you living in careless ease and drunkenness, and filled with the worries of this life. Don't let that day catch you unaware.

LUKE 21:34 NLT

Moderation and wisdom are traveling companions. If we are wise, we must learn to temper our appetites, our desires, and our impulses. When we do, we are blessed, in part, because God has created a world in which temperance is rewarded and intemperance is inevitably punished.

Would you like to improve your life and your self-esteem? Then harness your appetites and restrain your impulses. Moderation is difficult, of course; it is especially difficult in a prosperous society such as ours. But the rewards of moderation are numerous and long-lasting. Claim those rewards today.

No one can force you to moderate your appetites. The decision to live temperately (and wisely) is yours and yours alone. And so are the consequences.

2 minutes A Day

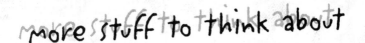
more stuff to think about

To many, total abstinence is easier
than perfect moderation.

AUGUSTINE OF HIPPO

We are all created differently.
We share a common need to balance
the different parts of our lives.

DR. WALT LARIMORE

When I feel like circumstances are spiraling downward
in my life, God taught me that whether I'm right side up
or upside down, I need to turn those circumstances over to
Him. He is the only one who can bring balance into my life.

CAROLE LEWIS

The Big Idea

When in doubt, be moderate. Moderation is wisdom in
action.

SELF-ESTEEM

Don't Fall in Love with Money

For the love of money is a root of all sorts of evil, and some by longing for it have wandered away from the faith and pierced themselves with many griefs. But flee from these things, you man of God, and pursue righteousness, godliness, faith, love, perseverance and gentleness.

1 TIMOTHY 6:11 NASB

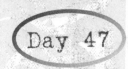

Our society is in love with money and the things that money can buy. God is not. God cares about people, not possessions, and so must we. We must, to the best of our abilities, love our neighbors as ourselves, and we must, to the best of our abilities, resist the mighty temptation to place possessions ahead of people.

Money, in and of itself, is not evil; worshipping money is. So today, as you prioritize matters of importance for you and yours, remember that God is almighty, but the dollar is not. If we worship God, we are blessed. But if we worship "the almighty dollar," we are inevitably punished because of our misplaced priorities—and our punishment inevitably comes sooner rather than later.

more stuff to think about

Theirs is an endless road, a hopeless maze,
who seek for goods before they seek for God.

BERNARD OF CLAIRVAUX

If you're unable to manage money, no job—
no matter how much it pays—pays enough.

CRISWELL FREEMAN

Money is a mirror that, strange as it sounds,
reflects our personal weaknesses and strengths
with amazing clarity.

DAVE RAMSEY

The Big Idea

You've heard it said that money can't buy happiness. Well,
it can't buy self-esteem, either. So, if you're trying to use
money to buy self-respect, forget about it. You can't buy self-
esteem in a store, so don't even try.

SELF-ESTEEM

Day 48

Keeping Life in Perspective

All I'm doing right now, friends, is showing how these things pertain to Apollos and me so that you will learn restraint and not rush into making judgments without knowing all the facts. It is important to look at things from God's point of view. I would rather not see you inflating or deflating reputations based on mere hearsay.

1 CORINTHIANS 4:6 MSG

Sometimes, amid the demands of daily life, we lose perspective. Life seems out of balance, and the pressures of everyday living seem overwhelming. What's needed is a fresh perspective, a restored sense of balance . . . and God.

If we call upon the Lord and seek to see the world through His eyes, He will give us guidance and wisdom and perspective. When we make God's priorities our priorities, He will lead us according to His plan and according to His commandments. When we trust God's plan and follow it, we feel better about ourselves and our service.

God's reality is the ultimate reality. May we all live accordingly.

more stuff to think about

Like a shadow declining swiftly…away…like the dew of
the morning gone with the heat of the day; like the wind in
the treetops, like a wave of the sea, so are our lives
on earth when seen in light of eternity.

RUTH BELL GRAHAM

I beg you do not squander life.
And don't live for this world only.

BILLY GRAHAM

When we look at the individual parts of our lives, some
things appear unfair and unpleasant. When we take them
out of the context of the big picture, we easily drift
into the attitude that we deserve better, and the tumble down
into the pit of pride begins.

SUSAN HUNT

The Big Idea

Keep life in perspective: Your life is an integral part of God's
grand plan. So don't become unduly upset over the minor
inconveniences of life, and don't worry too much about
today's setbacks—they're temporary.

SELF-ESTEEM

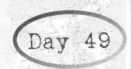

Don't Worry Too Much About Pleasing Everybody

Do you think I am trying to make people accept me?
No, God is the One I am trying to please.
Am I trying to please people? If I still wanted to please
people, I would not be a servant of Christ.

GALATIANS 1:10 NCV

Rick Warren observed, "Those who follow the crowd usually get lost in it." We know these words to be true, but oftentimes we fail to live by them. Instead of trusting God for guidance, we imitate our friends and suffer the consequences. Instead seeking to please our Father in heaven, we strive to please our peers, with decidedly mixed results.

Would you like a time-tested formula for building self-respect? Here is a formula that is proven and true: Seek God's approval first and other people's approval later. Does this sound too simple? Perhaps it is simple, but it is also the only way to reap the marvelous riches that God has in store for you.

Whom will you try to please today: your God or your friends? Your obligation is most certainly not to friends or even to family members. Your obligation is to an all-knowing, all-powerful God. You must seek to please Him first and always. No exceptions.

more stuff to think about

Pride opens the door to every other sin, for once we are more concerned with our reputation than our character, there is no end to the things we will do just to make ourselves "look good" before others.

WARREN WIERSBE

When we are set free from the bondage of pleasing others, when we are free from currying others' favor and others' approval—then no one will be able to make us miserable or dissatisfied. And then, if we know we have pleased God, contentment will be our consolation.

KAY ARTHUR

Those who, to please their listeners, avoid giving a forthright declaration of the will of God become slaves of those they would please and abandon the service of God.

BASIL THE GREAT

The Big Idea

If you are burdened with a "people-pleasing" personality, outgrow it. Realize that you can't please all of the people all of the time, nor should you attempt to.

SELF-ESTEEM

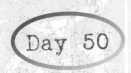

Think Ahead

I will instruct you and teach you in the way you should go;
I will guide you with My eye.

PSALM 32:8 NKJV

Maybe you've heard this old saying: "Look before you leap." Well, that saying may be old, but it still applies to you. Before you jump into something, you should look ahead and plan ahead. Otherwise, you might soon be sorry you jumped!

When you acquire the habit of thinking ahead and planning ahead, you'll make better choices (and, as a result, you'll feel better about yourself).

So, when it comes to the important things in life, don't allow impulsive behavior to ruin your future. Think long and hard about the consequences of your actions before you do something foolish . . . or dangerous . . . or both.

2 minutes A DAY

more stuff to think about

It's incredible to realize that what we do each day has meaning in the big picture of God's plan.

BILL HYBELS

Allow your dreams a place in your prayers and plans. God-given dreams can help you move into the future He is preparing for you.

BARBARA JOHNSON

The only way you can experience abundant life is to surrender your plans to Him.

CHARLES STANLEY

The Big Idea

Think ahead—it's the best way of making sure you don't get left behind.

SELF-ESTEEM

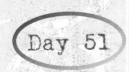

Day 51

Remember That Even If You Don't Love Yourself, God Does

Unfailing love surrounds those who trust the LORD.
PSALM 32:10 NLT

St. Augustine observed, "God loves each of us as if there were only one of us." Do you believe those words? Do you seek to have an intimate, one-on-one relationship with your Heavenly Father, or are you satisfied to keep Him at a "safe" distance?

God's love is bigger and more powerful than anybody (including you) can imagine, but His love is very real. So do yourself a favor right now: accept God's love with open arms and welcome His Son Jesus into your heart. And while you're at it, remember this: even when you don't love yourself very much, God still loves you. And God's right.

2 Minutes A Day

more stuff to think about

Our hearts have been made to cry out for a love
that can come only from our Creator.

ANGELA THOMAS

As I spent time with God, growing in my knowledge of Him
through prayer, Bible Study, obedience, and submission,
He would fill my life. And because God is love and because
He would fill me, His love would fill me.

ANNE GRAHAM LOTZ

When you agree to let God love the unlovely through you,
He never fails to make the unlovely lovely to you.

BETH MOORE

The Big Idea

God's love for you is too big to figure out, but it's not too
big to share. And the more you share God's love, the better
you'll feel about your world, your neighbors, and yourself.

SELF-ESTEEM

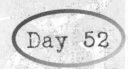

Keep Trying to Figure Out What God Has Planned for You

You will show me the path of life.
PSALM 16:11 NKJV

You'll feel better about yourself if you're living on purpose, not by accident. But sometimes that's hard to do. Why? Because God's plans aren't always clear. Sometimes we wander aimlessly in a wilderness of our own making. And sometimes, we struggle mightily against God in an unsuccessful attempt to find success and happiness through our own means, not His.

Are you genuinely trying to figure out God's purpose for your life? If so, you can be sure that with God's help, you will eventually discover it. So keep praying, and keep watching. And rest assured: God's got big plans for you . . . very big plans.

And when you discover those plans, you'll feel better about yourself . . . lots better.

more stuff to think about

If you want to give God a good laugh, tell Him your plans.

WILLARD SCOTT

He knows when we go into the storm, He watches over us in the storm, and He can bring us out of the storm when His purposes have been fulfilled.

WARREN WIERSBE

We forget that God sometimes has to say "No." We pray to Him as our heavenly Father, and like wise human fathers, He often says, "No," not from whim or caprice, but from wisdom, from love, and from knowing what is best for us.

PETER MARSHALL

The Big Idea

God has very big plans in store for your life, so trust Him and wait patiently for those plans to unfold. And remember: God's timing is best.

SELF-ESTEEM

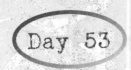

Warning: Some Media Messages Are Dangerous to Your Self-esteem

Do not love the world or the things in the world. If you love the world, the love of the Father is not in you.

1 JOHN 2:15 NCV

The media says that your appearance is all-important, that your clothes are all-important, that your car is all-important, and that partying is all-important. The media says that you need to be thinner, hipper, and sexier. The media says that it's cool to live on the edge, to live for the moment, and to push the envelope. But guess what? These messages are lies.

The "all-important" things in your life have little to do with parties, appearances, cars, clothes, or hipness. The all-important things in life have to do with your faith, your family, and your God. Period.

If you believe the media hype, you'll never feel very good about yourself because you'll never meet the media's standards. But you can meet God's standard by accepting His Son.

Whose standards will you try to meet today: the media's or God's? The answer should be simple . . . and hopefully, you'll get it right.

more stuff to think about

One of Satan's most effective ploys is to make us believe
that we are small, insignificant, and worthless.

SUSAN LENZKES

If you ever put a price tag on yourself, it would have to read
"Jesus" because that is what God paid to save you.

JOSH MCDOWELL

Human worth does not depend on beauty or intelligence or
accomplishments. We are all more valuable than
the possessions of the entire world simply
because God gave us that value.

JAMES DOBSON

The Big Idea

The media is sending out messages that are dangerous to
your physical, emotional, and spiritual health. If you choose
to believe those messages, you're setting yourself up for lots
of trouble.

SELF-ESTEEM

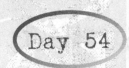

Change Your Thoughts and Change Your Life

May the words of my mouth and the thoughts of my heart be pleasing to you, O Lord, my rock and my redeemer.
Psalm 19:14 NLT

Thoughts are intensely powerful things. Your thoughts have the power to lift you up or drag you down; they have the power to energize you or deplete you, to inspire you to greater accomplishments or to make those accomplishments impossible.

The Bible teaches you to guard your thoughts against things that are hurtful or wrong (Proverbs 4:23). Yet, sometimes you'll be tempted to let your thoughts run wild, especially if those thoughts are of the negative variety.

If you've acquired the habit of thinking constructively about yourself and your circumstances, congratulations. But if you're mired in the mental quicksand of overly self-critical thoughts, it's time to change your thoughts . . . and your life.

Your thoughts can build up your self-esteem, or they can destroy it. So think carefully—very carefully—about the way you think.

2 minutes A DAY

more stuff to think about

Attitude is the mind's paintbrush; it can color any situation.

BARBARA JOHNSON

Every major spiritual battle is in the mind.

CHARLES STANLEY

It is the thoughts and intents of the heart
that shape a person's life.

JOHN ELDREDGE

The Big Idea

Good thoughts create good deeds. Good thoughts lead to
good deeds and bad thoughts lead elsewhere. So guard
your thoughts accordingly.

SELF-ESTEEM

Behave Yourself

Exercise your freedom by serving God,
not by breaking rules.
1 PETER 2:16 MSG

Okay, answer this question honestly: Do you behave differently because of your relationship with Jesus? Or do you behave in pretty much the same way that you would if you weren't a believer? Hopefully, the fact that you've invited Christ to reign over your heart means that you've made BIG changes in your thoughts and your actions.

Doing the right thing is not always easy, especially when you're tired or frustrated. But, doing the wrong thing almost always leads to trouble (and, eventually, to poor self-esteem).

So, if you want to feel good about yourself, don't follow the crowd—follow Jesus. And keep following Him every day of your life.

more stuff to think about

People who do not develop and practice good thinking often find themselves at the mercy of their circumstances.

JOHN MAXWELL

Holiness is not inability to sin, but ability not to sin.

G. CAMPBELL MORGAN

It is by acts and not by ideas that people live.

HARRY EMERSON FOSDICK

The Big Idea

Ask yourself if your behavior has been changed by your unfolding relationship with God. If the answer to this question is unclear to you—or if the honest answer is a resounding no—think of a single step you can take, a positive change in your life, that will bring you closer to your Creator. When you take even one positive step, you'll feel better about yourself.

SELF-ESTEEM

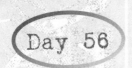

Become Sold on Yourself

*You're blessed when you're content with just who you are—
no more, no less. That's the moment you find yourselves
proud owners of everything that can't be bought.*

<small>MATTHEW 5:5 MSG</small>

D o you place a high value on your talents, your time,
your capabilities, and your opportunities? If so,
congratulations. But if you've acquired the insidious
habit of devaluing your time, your work, or yourself, it's now
time for a change.

Pearl Bailey correctly observed, "The first and worst of all
frauds is to cheat one's self. All sin is easy after that."

If you've been squandering opportunities or selling
yourself short, it's time to rethink the way that you think
about yourself and your opportunities. No one can seize
those opportunities for you, and no one can build up your
self-confidence if you're unwilling to believe in yourself. So, if
you've been talking yourself down, stop. You deserve better.
And if you don't give yourself healthy respect, who will?

more stuff to think about

I may have tasted peace, but to believe that the God of heaven and earth calls me beautiful—well, I think I could rest in that. If I truly knew that He was smitten with me, maybe I could take a deep breath, square my shoulders, and go out to face the world with confidence.

ANGELA THOMAS

God knows all that is true about us and is a friend to the face we show and the face we hide.
He does not love us less for our human weaknesses.

SHEILA WALSH

Do not wish to be anything but what you are, and try to be that perfectly.

ST. FRANCIS OF SALES

The Big Idea

Don't drive yourself crazy worrying about self-esteem. Instead, worry more about living a life that is pleasing to God. Learn to think optimistically. Find a worthy purpose. Find people to love and people to serve. When you do, your self-esteem will, on most days, take care of itself.

SELF-ESTEEM

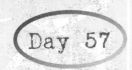

Hang Out
with Positive People

As iron sharpens iron, so people can improve each other.
PROVERBS 27:17 NCV

If you hang out with positive people, you feel better about yourself—if you don't, you won't. So why not choose friends who help you feel better about yourself, not worse?

And as you're thinking about the kind of friends who can make a positive impact on your life, here's something else worth considering: pessimism and Christianity don't mix. Why? Because Christians have every reason to be optimistic about life here on earth and life eternal.

Mrs. Charles E. Cowman advised, "Never yield to gloomy anticipation. Place your hope and confidence in God. He has no record of failure." Yet sometimes, despite our trust in God, we may fall into the spiritual traps of worry, frustration, anxiety, or sheer exhaustion, and our hearts become troubled. What's needed is plenty of rest, a large dose of perspective, God's healing touch . . . and a heaping helping of encouragement from upbeat Christian friends.

more stuff to think about

We urgently need people who encourage and inspire us to move toward God and away from the world's enticing pleasures.

JIM CYMBALA

Though I know intellectually how vulnerable I am to pride and power, I am the last one to know when I succumb to their seduction. That's why spiritual Lone Rangers are so dangerous—and why we must depend on trusted brothers and sisters who love us enough to tell us the truth.

CHUCK COLSON

Satan watches for those vessels that sail without convoy.

GEORGE SWINNOCK

The Big Idea

If you choose friends who behave themselves . . . you'll be far more likely to behave yourself, too. And when you do, you'll feel better about your friends and yourself.

SELF-ESTEEM

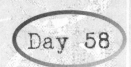

Day 58

Decide Whose Opinions Matter Most

Our only goal is to please God whether we live here or there, because we must all stand before Christ to be judged.
2 CORINTHIANS 5:9-10 NCV

What other people think of you should be relatively unimportant; however, God's view of you—His understanding of your actions, your thoughts, and your motivations—should be vitally important.

Few things in life are more futile than "keeping up appearances" for the sake of other people. What is important, of course, is pleasing your Father in heaven. You please Him when your intentions are pure and your actions are just.

So do yourself a big-time favor: don't worry too much about the way that you appear to other people. Worry, instead, about how you appear to God. When you do, you'll respect yourself more. Lot's more.

more stuff to think about

It is impossible to please God doing things motivated by and produced by the flesh.

BILL BRIGHT

You must never sacrifice your relationship with God for the sake of a relationship with another person.

CHARLES STANLEY

It is impossible to please everybody. It's not impossible to please God. So try pleasing God.

CRISWELL FREEMAN

The Big Idea

Remember that being obedient to God means that you cannot always please other people. So focus on your relationship with God. When you do, you'll find that every other relationship and every other aspect of your life will be more fulfilling.

SELF-ESTEEM

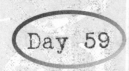

Worship God, Not the World

You shall have no other gods before Me.
Exodus 20:3 NKJV

In Exodus 20:3, God makes it clear that we must have no other gods before Him. Yet the world tempts us to do otherwise. The world is a noisy, distracting place, a place that offers countless temptations and dangers. The world seems to cry, "Worship me with your time, your money, your energy, your thoughts, and your life!" But if we are wise, we won't fall prey to that temptation.

Are you putting God first in every aspect of your life? If so, you'll feel better about your friends, your future, your world, and yourself. So today and every day, be sure to worship God first and everything else next. No exceptions.

more stuff to think about

Too many Christians have geared their program to please,
to entertain, and to gain favor from this world.
We are concerned with how much, instead of how little,
like this age we can become.

BILLY GRAHAM

Our joy ends where love of the world begins.

C. H. SPURGEON

Aim at heaven and you will get earth thrown in;
aim at earth and you will get neither.

C. S. LEWIS

The Big Idea

Seek, discover, and follow God's will. If you seek the things
that God values, you will be satisfied; if you seek the things
that the world values, you will be disappointed.

SELF-ESTEEM

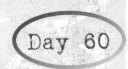

Don't Be a Halfhearted Christian

*You who are trying to follow God and the world
at the same time, make your thinking pure.*

JAMES 4:8 NCV

If you're willing to stand up for the things you believe in, you'll feel better about yourself and you'll make better choices. But if you're one person on Sunday morning and a different person throughout the rest of the week, you'll be doing yourself—and your conscience—a big disservice.

The moment that you decide to stand up for your beliefs, you can no longer be a lukewarm, halfhearted Christian. And, when you are no longer a lukewarm Christian, God rejoices (and the devil doesn't).

So stand up for your beliefs. And remember this: in the battle of good versus evil, the devil never takes a day off . . . and neither should you.

2 minutes A DAY

more stuff to think about

The world's sewage system threatens to contaminate
the stream of Christian thought.
Is the world shaping your mind, or is Christ?

BILLY GRAHAM

We become whatever we are committed to.

RICK WARREN

Christianity, if false, is of no importance, and,
if true, of infinite importance. The one thing it cannot be
is moderately important.

C. S. LEWIS

The Big Idea

Don't be embarrassed to discuss your faith. You need not
have attended seminary to have worthwhile opinions. When
it comes to your faith, let the world know where you stand.

SELF-ESTEEM

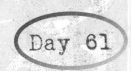

Watch Your Words

*When you talk, do not say harmful things, but say what
people need—words that will help others become stronger.
Then what you say will do good to those who listen to you.*

EPHESIANS 4:29 NCV

You'll feel better about yourself if you pay careful
attention to the words you speak. So today, as you
fulfill the responsibilities that God has placed before
you, ask yourself this question: "Do my words and deeds
bear witness to the ultimate Truth that God has placed in
my heart, or am I allowing the pressures of everyday life
to overwhelm me?" It's a big question that only you can
answer.

Of course you must never take the Lord's name in vain,
but it doesn't stop there. You must also strive to speak words
of encouragement, words that lift others up, words that give
honor to your Heavenly Father.

The Bible clearly warns that you will be judged by the
words you speak, so choose those words carefully. And
remember: God is always listening.

more stuff to think about

When you talk, choose the very same words that you would use if Jesus were looking over your shoulder. Because He is.

MARIE T. FREEMAN

Attitude and the spirit in which we communicate are as important as the words we say.

CHARLES STANLEY

The things that we feel most deeply we ought to learn to be silent about, at least until we have talked them over thoroughly with God.

ELISABETH ELLIOT

The Big Idea

Cool off before you spout off. If you're too angry to have a conversation that is both loving and constructive, put things on hold until you simmer down.

SELF-ESTEEM

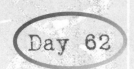

Take Worship Seriously

Happy are those who hear the joyful call to worship,
for they will walk in the light of your presence, LORD.
PSALM 89:15 NLT

D o you want to feel better about yourself? Then make sure that you worship God every day of your life, not just on Sunday.

Do you take time each day to worship your Father in heaven, or do you wait until Sunday morning to praise Him for His blessings? The answer to this question will, in large part, determine the quality and direction of your spiritual life.

When we worship God every day of our lives, we are blessed. When we fail to worship God, for whatever reason, we forfeit the spiritual gifts that He intends for us.

Every day provides opportunities to put God where He belongs: at the center of our lives. When we do so, we worship Him not only with our words, but also with our deeds, and that's as it should be. For believers, God comes first. Always first.

2 minutes a day

more stuff to think about

In Biblical worship you do not find the repetition of a phrase;
instead, you find the worshipers rehearsing the character of
God and His ways, reminding Him of His faithfulness
and His wonderful promises.

KAY ARTHUR

If anyone should ask a truly wise man why he was born,
he will answer without fear or hesitation, that he was born
for the purpose of worshiping God.

LACTANTIUS

Worship is a daunting task. Each worships differently.
But each should worship.

MAX LUCADO

The Big Idea

Worship reminds you of the awesome power of God. So
worship Him daily, and allow Him to work through you every
day of the week (not just on Sunday).

SELF-ESTEEM

Be a Joyful Christian

Make me hear joy and gladness.
PSALM 51:8 NKJV

Have you made the choice to rejoice? Hopefully so. After all, if you're a believer, you have plenty of reasons to be joyful. Yet sometimes, amid the inevitable hustle and bustle of life here on earth, you may lose sight of your blessings as you wrestle with the challenges of everyday life.

Psalm 100 reminds us that, as believers, we have every reason to celebrate: "Shout for joy to the LORD, all the earth. Worship the LORD with gladness" (vv. 1-2 NIV). Yet sometimes, we can forfeit—albeit temporarily—the joy that God intends for our lives.

If you find yourself feeling discouraged or worse, it's time to slow down and have a quiet conversation with your Creator. If your heart is heavy, open the door of your soul to the Father and to His only begotten Son. Christ offers you His peace and His joy. Accept it and share it freely, just as Christ has freely shared His joy with you.

more stuff to think about

In the absence of all other joys,
the joy of the Lord can fill the soul to the brim.

C. H. SPURGEON

According to Jesus, it is God's will that His children
be filled with the joy of life.

CATHERINE MARSHALL

Joy has nothing to do with circumstances. Joy is a choice.
It is a matter of attitude that stems from
one's confidence in God.

CHARLES SWINDOLL

The Big Idea

When you experience God's joy for yourself, you'll feel
differently about everything, including yourself.

SELF-ESTEEM

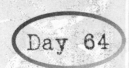
Make the Most of Your Talents

Do not neglect the spiritual gift that is within you . . . .
1 TIMOTHY 4:14 NASB

Face it: you've got an array of talents that need to be refined—and you'll feel better about yourself when you refine them. But nobody will force you to do the hard work of converting raw talent into prime-time talent. That's a job you must do for yourself.

Today, make a promise to yourself that you will earnestly seek to discover the talents that God has given you. Then, nourish those talents and make them grow. Finally, vow to share your gifts with the world for as long as God gives you the power to do so. When you do, you'll feel better about yourself and your abilities . . . and the world will, too.

2 minutes A DAY

more stuff to think about

Employ whatever God has entrusted you with,
in doing good, all possible good,
in every possible kind and degree.

JOHN WESLEY

God often reveals His direction for our lives through
the way He made us…with a certain personality
and unique skills.

BILL HYBELS

If you want to reach your potential, you need to add
a strong work ethic to your talent.

JOHN MAXWELL

The Big Idea

You have special abilities that can be nurtured carefully or
ignored totally. The challenge, of course, is to do the former
and to avoid the latter.

SELF-ESTEEM

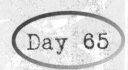

Encourage Other People

*So then, we must pursue what promotes peace
and what builds up one another.*
ROMANS 14:19 HOLMAN CSB

Want to feel better about yourself? Then start encouraging other people to feel good about themselves.

In Ephesians, Paul advises, "Do not let any unwholesome talk come out of your mouths, but only what is helpful for building others up according to their needs, that it may benefit those who listen" (4:29 NIV). Paul's words still apply.

Your friends and family members probably need more encouragement and less criticism. The same can be said for you. So be a booster, not a cynic—and find friends who do likewise.

2 minutes A DAY

more stuff to think about

We would all much better mend our ways if we were
as ready to pray for one another as we are to offer
one another reproach and rebuke.

St. Thomas More

A lot of people have gone further than they thought
they could because someone else thought they could.

Zig Ziglar

The overall goal in helping any individual is to communicate
hope, that they might more courageously and confidently
face daily life with its trials and struggles.

Verna Birkey

The Big Idea

When you help other people feel better about themselves,
you'll feel better about yourself, too. So what are you waiting
for?

SELF-ESTEEM

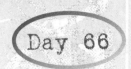

Guard Your Heart and Mind

Summing it all up, friends, I'd say you'll do best by filling your minds and meditating on things true, noble, reputable, authentic, compelling, gracious, the best, not the worst; the beautiful, not the ugly; things to praise, not things to curse. Put into practice what you learned from me, what you heard and saw and realized. Do that, and God, who makes everything work together, will work you into his most excellent harmonies.

PHILIPPIANS 4:8-9 MSG

You are near and dear to God. He loves you more than you can imagine, and He wants the very best for you. And one more thing: God wants you to guard your heart.

Every day, you are faced with choices . . . lots of them. You can do the right thing, or not. You can tell the truth, or not. You can be kind and generous and obedient. Or not.

Today, the world will offer you countless opportunities to let down your guard and, by doing so, let the devil do his worst. Be watchful and obedient. Guard your heart by giving it to your Heavenly Father; it is safe with Him.

2 MINUTES A DAY

more stuff to think about

Prayer guards hearts and minds and causes God
to bring peace out of chaos.

BETH MOORE

God meant that we adjust to the Gospel—
not the other way around.

VANCE HAVNER

Our actions disclose what goes on within us, just as its fruit
makes known a tree otherwise unknown to us.

THALASSIOS THE LIBAN

The Big Idea

You live in a society where temptations are everywhere. Your
job is to aggressively avoid those temptations before the
devil can get his hooks into you.

SELF-ESTEEM

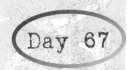

Be Kind to Everybody

And be kind and compassionate to one another, forgiving one another, just as God also forgave you in Christ.

EPHESIANS 4:32 HOLMAN CSB

Would you like an ironclad formula for improved self-esteem? Try this: be kind to everybody.

Kindness is a choice. Sometimes, when you feel happy or generous, you may find it easy to be kind. Other times, when you are discouraged or tired, you can scarcely summon the energy to utter a single kind word. But, God's commandment is clear: He intends that you make the conscious choice to treat others with kindness and respect, no matter your circumstances, no matter your emotions.

So today, spread a heaping helping of kindness wherever you go. When you do, you'll discover that the more kindness you give away to others, the more you'll receive in return.

2 MINUTES A DAY

more stuff to think about

Every word we speak, every action we take, has an effect on the totality of humanity. No one can escape that privilege—or that responsibility.

LAURIE BETH JONES

As you're rushing through life, take time to stop a moment, look into people's eyes, say something kind, and try to make them laugh!

BARBARA JOHNSON

As much as God loves to hear our worship and adoration, surely he delights all the more in seeing our gratitude translated into simple kindnesses that keep the chain of praise unbroken, alive in others' hearts.

EVELYN CHRISTENSON

The Big Idea

The Golden Rule starts with you, so when in doubt, be a little kinder than necessary. You'll feel better about yourself when you do.

SELF-ESTEEM

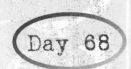

Don't Be Too Judgmental

Stop judging others, and you will not be judged.
Stop criticizing others, or it will all come back on you.
If you forgive others, you will be forgiven.

LUKE 6:37 NLT

Here's something worth thinking about: If you judge other people harshly, God will judge you in the same fashion. But that's not all (thank goodness!). The Bible also promises that if you forgive others, you, too, will be forgiven. Have you developed the bad habit of behaving yourself like an amateur judge and jury, assigning blame and condemnation wherever you go? If so, it's time to grow up and obey God. When it comes to judging everything and everybody, God doesn't need your help . . . and He doesn't want it.

more stuff to think about

Christians think they are prosecuting attorneys or judges,
when, in reality, God has called all of us to be witnesses.

WARREN WIERSBE

Don't judge other people more harshly
than you want God to judge you.

MARIE T. FREEMAN

Turn your attention upon yourself and beware of judging
the deeds of other men, for in judging others a man labors
vainly, often makes mistakes, and easily sins; whereas, in
judging and taking stock of himself he does something
that is always profitable.

THOMAS À KEMPIS

The Big Idea

Your ability to judge others requires a divine insight that you
simply don't have. So do everybody (including yourself) a
favor: don't judge.

SELF-ESTEEM

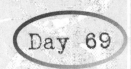

Day 69

Depend Upon God's Protection

Finally, be strong in the Lord and in his mighty power.
Put on the full armor of God so that you can take your stand
against the devil's schemes.

EPHESIANS 6:10-11 NIV

In a world filled with dangers and temptations, God is the ultimate armor. In a world filled with misleading messages, God's Word is the ultimate truth. In a world filled with more frustrations than we can count, God's Son offers the ultimate peace. Will you accept God's peace and wear God's armor against the dangers of our world?

Sometimes, in the crush of everyday life, God may seem far away, but He is not. God is everywhere you have ever been and everywhere you will ever go. He is with you night and day; He knows your thoughts and your prayers. He is your ultimate Protector. And, when you earnestly seek His protection, you will find it because He is here—always—waiting patiently for you to reach out to Him.

2 MINUTES A DAY

more stuff to think about

He is within and without. His Spirit dwells within me.
His armor protects me. He goes before me
and is behind me.

MARY MORRISON SUGGS

It is faith that what happens to me matters to God as well as
to me that gives me joy, that promises me that I am eternally
the subject of God's compassion, and that assures me that
the compassion was manifested most brilliantly when
God came to us in a stable in Bethlehem.

MADELEINE L'ENGLE

Under heaven's lock and key, we are protected by the most
efficient security system available: the power of God.

CHARLES SWINDOLL

The Big Idea

If you'd like infinite protection, there's only one place you
can receive it: from an infinite God. So remember: when you
live in the center of God's will, you will also be living in the
center of God's protection.

SELF-ESTEEM

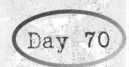

Keep Making Choices That Are Pleasing to God

I am offering you life or death, blessings or curses.
Now, choose life! Then you and your children may live.
To choose life is to love the Lord your God, obey him,
and stay close to him.

DEUTERONOMY 30:19-20 NCV

Because we are creatures of free will, we make choices—lots of them. When we make choices that are pleasing to our Heavenly Father, we are blessed. When we make choices that cause us to walk in the footsteps of God's Son, we feel better about ourselves and we enjoy the abundance that Christ has promised to those who follow Him. But when we make choices that are displeasing to God, we sow seeds that have the potential to bring forth a bitter harvest.

Today, as you encounter the challenges of everyday living, you will make hundreds of choices. Choose wisely. Make your thoughts and your actions pleasing to God. And remember: every choice that is displeasing to Him is the wrong choice—no exceptions.

more stuff to think about

Life is a series of choices between the bad, the good, and the best. Everything depends on how we choose.

VANCE HAVNER

God is voting for us all the time. The devil is voting against us all the time. The way we vote carries the election.

CORRIE TEN BOOM

Commitment to His lordship on Easter, at revivals, or even every Sunday is not enough. We must choose this day— and every day—whom we will serve. This deliberate act of the will is the inevitable choice between habitual fellowship and habitual failure.

BETH MOORE

The Big Idea

Wise choices build self-confidence. Unwise choices don't. So choose wisely.

SELF-ESTEEM

Keep Searching for Wisdom

If you don't know what you're doing, pray to the Father. He loves to help. You'll get his help, and won't be condescended to when you ask for it. Ask boldly, believingly, without a second thought. People who "worry their prayers" are like wind-whipped waves. Don't think you're going to get anything from the Master that way, adrift at sea, keeping all your options open.

JAMES 1:5-8 MSG

Do you seek the wisdom that only God can give? If so, ask Him for it! If you ask God for guidance, He will not withhold it. If you petition Him sincerely, and if you genuinely seek to form a relationship with Him, your Heavenly Father will guide your steps and enlighten your heart. But be forewarned: You will not acquire God's wisdom without obeying His commandments. Why? Because God's wisdom is more than just a collection of thoughts; it is, first and foremost, a way of life.

Wisdom is as wisdom does. So, if you sincerely seek God's wisdom, don't be satisfied to learn something; make up your mind to become something. And then, as you allow God to remake you in the image of His Son, you will most surely become wise.

more stuff to think about

Ask the God who made you to keep remaking you.
NORMAN VINCENT PEALE

The more wisdom enters our hearts, the more we will be
able to trust our hearts in difficult situations.
JOHN ELDREDGE

Wisdom always waits for the right time to act,
while emotion always pushes for action right now.
JOYCE MEYER

The Big Idea

Need wisdom? God's got it. If you want it, then study God's
Word and associate with godly people.

SELF-ESTEEM

Day 72

Aim High

I can do everything through him that gives me strength.
PHILIPPIANS 4:13 NIV

Are you willing to dream big dreams? Hopefully so; after all, God promises that we can do "all things" through Him. Yet most of us, even the most devout among us, live far below our potential. We take half measures; we dream small dreams; we waste precious time and energy on the distractions of the world. But God has other plans for us. Our Creator intends that we live faithfully, hopefully, courageously, and abundantly. He knows that we are capable of so much more; and He wants us to do the things we're capable of doing; and He wants us to start doing those things now.

more stuff to think about

You cannot out-dream God.

JOHN ELDREDGE

Always stay connected to people and seek out things that bring you joy. Dream with abandon. Pray confidently.

BARBARA JOHNSON

Set goals so big that unless God helps you, you will be a miserable failure.

BILL BRIGHT

The Big Idea

Making your dreams come true requires work. John Maxwell writes, "The gap between your vision and your present reality can only be filled through a commitment to maximize your potential." Enough said.

SELF-ESTEEM

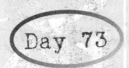

Don't Overestimate the Size of Your Problems

Ah Lord GOD! Behold, You have made the heavens and the earth by Your great power and by Your outstretched arm! Nothing is too difficult for You.

JEREMIAH 32:17 NASB

If a temporary loss of perspective has left you worried, exhausted, or both, it's time to readjust your thought patterns. Negative thoughts are habit-forming; thankfully, so are positive ones. With practice, you can form the habit of focusing on God's priorities and your possibilities. When you do, you'll soon discover that you will spend less time fretting about your challenges and more time praising God for His gifts.

When you call upon the Lord and prayerfully seek His will, He will give you wisdom and perspective. When you make God's priorities your priorities, He will direct your steps and calm your fears. So, today and every day hereafter, pray for a sense of balance and perspective. And remember: No problems are too big for God—and that includes yours.

2 minutes A DAY

more stuff to think about

God has plans—not problems—for our lives.

CORRIE TEN BOOM

Instead of being frustrated and overwhelmed by all that is
going on in our world, go to the Lord and ask Him
to give you His eternal perspective.

KAY ARTHUR

The Bible is a remarkable commentary on perspective.
Through its divine message, we are brought face to face with
issues and tests in daily living and how, by the power of the
Holy Spirit, we are enabled to respond positively to them.

LUCI SWINDOLL

The Big Idea

Problem-solving 101: When it comes to solving problems,
work beats worry. Remember: It is better to fix than to fret.

SELF-ESTEEM

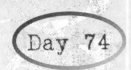

Do First Things First

Therefore, get your minds ready for action,
being self-disciplined . . . .
1 PETER 1:13 HOLMAN CSB

"First things first." These words are easy to speak but hard to put into practice. For busy people living in a demanding world, placing first things first can be difficult indeed. Why? Because so many people are expecting so many things from us!

If you're having trouble prioritizing your day, perhaps you've been trying to organize your life according to your own plans, not God's. A better strategy, of course, is to take your daily obligations and place them in the hands of the One who created you. To do so, you must prioritize your day according to God's commandments, and you must seek His will and His wisdom in all matters. Then, you can face the day with the assurance that the same God who created our universe out of nothingness will help you place first things first in your own life.

Do you feel overwhelmed or confused? Turn the concerns of this day over to God—prayerfully, earnestly, and often. Then, listen for His answer . . . and trust the answer He gives.

more stuff to think about

Blessed are those who know what on earth they are here on earth to do and set themselves about the business of doing it.

MAX LUCADO

No test of a man's true character is more conclusive than how he spends his time and his money.

PATRICK MORLEY

Does God care about all the responsibilities we have to juggle in our daily lives? Of course. But he cares more that our lives demonstrate balance, the ability to discern what is essential and give ourselves fully to it.

PENELOPE STOKES

The Big Idea

Unless you put first things first, you're bound to finish last. And that means putting God first.

SELF-ESTEEM

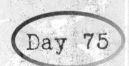
Build Positive Friendships

Light shines on those who do right;
joy belongs to those who are honest. Rejoice in the Lord,
you who do right. Praise his holy name.

PSALM 97:11-12 NCV

If you'd like to build a positive life, find positive friends. If you'd like to live a godly life, seek the fellowship of godly friends. If you'd like to live passionately, prayerfully, and purposefully, spend time with people who are already living passionate, prayerful, purposeful lives. Soon, you'll discover that you will inevitably become more and more like the people who surround you day in and day out.

In choosing your friends, you set your course for the future. So choose carefully . . . very carefully.

more stuff to think about

For better or worse, you will eventually become more and
more like the people you associate with.
So why not associate with people who
make you better, not worse?

MARIE T. FREEMAN

The effective mentor strives to help a man or woman
discover what they can be in Christ and then holds
them accountable to become that person.

HOWARD HENDRICKS

Yes, the Spirit was sent to be our Counselor.
Yes, Jesus speaks to us personally. But often he works
through another human being.

JOHN ELDREDGE

The Big Idea

Positive friends will help you build a healthier self-image.
So if you want to feel better about yourself, hang out with
positive friends, not cynical ones.

SELF-ESTEEM

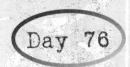

Day 76

Have the Courage to Risk Failure

The fear of human opinion disables;
trusting in God protects you from that.
PROVERBS 29:25 MSG

As we consider the uncertainties of the future, we are confronted with a powerful temptation: the temptation to "play it safe." Unwilling to move mountains, we fret over molehills. Unwilling to entertain great hopes for the tomorrow, we focus on the unfairness of the today. Unwilling to trust God completely, we take timid half-steps when God intends that we make giant leaps.

Today, ask God for the courage to step beyond the boundaries of your doubts. Ask Him to guide you to a place where you can realize your full potential—a place where you are freed from the fear of failure. Ask Him to do His part, and promise Him that you will do your part. Don't ask Him to lead you to a "safe" place; ask Him to lead you to the "right" place . . . and remember: those two places are seldom the same.

2 minutes A DAY

How beautiful it is to learn that grace isn't fragile,
and that in the family of God we can fail
and not be a failure.

GLORIA GAITHER

Leave nothing undared for the Kingdom of God.

ST. EUGENE DE MAZENOD

Let us arm ourselves against our spiritual enemies
with courage. They think twice about engaging
with one who fights boldly.

ST. JOHN CLIMACUS

The Big Idea

If you're too afraid of failure, you may not live up to your
potential. Remember that failing isn't nearly as bad as failing
to try.

SELF-ESTEEM

Don't Overestimate the Importance of Stuff

And He told them, "Watch out and be on guard against all greed, because one's life is not in the abundance of his possessions."

LUKE 12:15 HOLMAN CSB

How important are our material possessions? Not as important as we might think. In a well-balanced life, material possessions should play a rather small role. Of course, we all need the basic necessities of life, but once we meet those needs for ourselves and for our families, the piling up of possessions often creates more problems than it solves. Our real riches are not of this world. We are never really rich until we are rich in spirit.

If you've become preoccupied with money and the things that money can buy, it's time to de-emphasize things material and re-emphasize things spiritual. When you do, you'll feel better about yourself . . . and you'll begin storing up riches that will endure forever: the spiritual kind.

more stuff to think about

A society that pursues pleasure runs the risk of raising
expectations ever higher, so that true contentment
always lies tantalizingly out of reach.

PHILIP YANCEY AND PAUL BRAND

It's sobering to contemplate how much time, effort, sacrifice,
compromise, and attention we give to acquiring and
increasing our supply of something that is totally
insignificant in eternity.

ANNE GRAHAM LOTZ

The more we stuff ourselves with material pleasures,
the less we seem to appreciate life.

BARBARA JOHNSON

The Big Idea

Too much stuff? Beware. Too much stuff doesn't ensure
happiness or build lasting self-esteem. In fact, having too
much stuff can actually prevent happiness.

SELF-ESTEEM

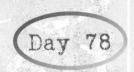

Keep Learning Every Day

*It takes knowledge to fill a home with rare
and beautiful treasures.*

PROVERBS 24:4 NCV

Another way to feel better about yourself is to keep acquiring both knowledge and wisdom. Knowledge is found in textbooks. Wisdom, on the other hand, is found in God's Holy Word and in the carefully-chosen words of loving parents, family members, and friends.

Knowledge is an important building block in a well-lived life, and it pays rich dividends both personally and professionally. But, wisdom is even more important because it refashions not only the mind, but also the heart.

When you study God's Word and live according to His commandments, you will become wise . . . and you will be a blessing to your family and to the world.

more stuff to think about

The wonderful thing about God's schoolroom is that
we get to grade our own papers. You see, He doesn't
test us so He can learn how well we're doing.
He tests us so we can discover how well we're doing.

CHARLES SWINDOLL

Today is yesterday's pupil.

THOMAS FULLER

The Big Idea

Keep learning. The future belongs to those who are willing to
do the work that's required to prepare for it.

SELF-ESTEEM

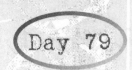

Return God's Love by Sharing It

*My dear, dear friends, if God loved us like this,
we certainly ought to love each other.*
1 JOHN 4:11 MSG

God loves you. How will you respond to His love? The Bible clearly defines what your response should be: "You shall love the Lord your God with all your heart, with all your soul, and with all your strength" (Deuteronomy 6:5 NKJV). But you must not stop there. You must also love your neighbor as yourself. Jesus teaches that "On these two commandments hang all the Law and the Prophets" (Matthew 22:40).

Today, as you meet the demands of everyday living, will you pause long enough to return God's love? And then will you share it? Prayerfully, you will. When you embrace God's love, you are forever changed. When you embrace God's love, you feel differently about yourself, your family, your friends, and your world. When you embrace God's love, you have enough love to keep and enough love to share: enough love for a day, enough love for a lifetime, enough love for all eternity.

2 minutes A DAY

more stuff to think about

He who is filled with love is filled with God Himself.

AUGUSTINE OF HIPPO

Although our actions have nothing to do with gaining our own salvation, they might be used by God to save somebody else! What we do really matters, and it can affect the eternities of people we care about.

BILL HYBELS

Being an effective witness means that we call attention to our testimony and leave the results to Him.

CALVIN MILLER

The Big Idea

Be creative: There are many ways to say, "I love you." Find them. Use them. And keep using them.

SELF-ESTEEM

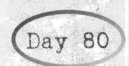

Be Patient with Others and with Yourself

God has chosen you and made you his holy people.
He loves you. So always do these things: Show mercy to
others, be kind, humble, gentle, and patient.

COLOSSIANS 3:12 NCV

The dictionary defines the word *patience* as "the ability to be calm, tolerant, and understanding." If that describes you, you can skip the rest of this page. But, if you're like most of us, you'd better keep reading.

For most of us, patience is a hard thing to master. Why? Because we have lots of things we want, and we want them NOW (if not sooner). But the Bible tells us that we must learn to wait patiently for the things that God has in store for us.

The next time you find your patience tested to the limit, remember that the world unfolds according to God's timetable, not yours. Sometimes, you must wait patiently, and that's as it should be. After all, think how patient God has been with you!

2 minutes a day

more stuff to think about

All things pass. Patience attains all it strives for.

ST. TERESA OF AVILA

Patient waiting is often the highest way of doing God's will.

ST. FRANCIS DE SALES

The Big Idea

God has been patient with you . . . now it's your turn to be patient with others and with yourself.

SELF-ESTEEM

Keep Growing Spiritually

*So let us stop going over the basics of Christianity
again and again. Let us go on instead
and become mature in our understanding.*
HEBREWS 6:1 NLT

Are you a fully-grown person? Physically: maybe so.
But spiritually? No way! And thank goodness that
you're not! Even if you're very mature for your age,
you've still got lots of room to grow.

The 19th-century writer Hannah Whitall Smith observed,
"The maturity of a Christian experience cannot be reached
in a moment." No kidding. In truth, the search for spiritual
growth lasts a lifetime.

When we cease to grow, either emotionally or spiritually,
we do ourselves and our families a profound disservice. But,
if we study God's Word, if we obey His commandments, and
if we live in the center of His will, we will not be "stagnant"
believers; we will, instead, be growing Christians . . . and
that's exactly what God wants for our lives. Come to think of
it, that's exactly what you should want, too.

2 minutes A DAY

more stuff to think about

People should think less about what they ought to do,
and more about what they ought to be. If only their living
were good, their work would shine forth brightly.

MEISTER ECKHART

If you're seeking God's will for your life,
you'll probably need to look outside your comfort zone.

CRISWELL FREEMAN

Approach the Scriptures not so much as a manual of
Christian principles but as the testimony of God's friends
on what it means to walk with him through
a thousand different episodes.

JOHN ELDREDGE

The Big Idea

If you're determined to keep growing spiritually, you'll feel
better about your world, your faith, and yourself. So keep
growing . . . or else.

SELF-ESTEEM

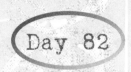

Learn to Accept Your Mistakes

*LORD, help! they cried in their trouble,
and he saved them from their distress.*

PSALM 107:13 NLT

Mistakes: nobody likes 'em but everybody makes 'em. Sometimes, even if you're a very good person, you're going to mess things up. And when you do, God is always ready to forgive you—He'll do His part, but you should be willing to do your part, too. Here's what you need to do:

1. If you've been engaging in behavior that is against the will of God, cease and desist (that means stop).
2. If you made a mistake, learn from it and don't repeat it (that's called getting smarter).
3. If you've hurt somebody, apologize and ask for forgiveness (that's called doing the right thing).
4. Ask for God's forgiveness, too (He'll give it whenever you ask, but you do need to ask!).

Have you made a mistake? If so, today is the perfect day to make things right with everybody (and the word "everybody" includes yourself, your family, your friends, and your God).

Mistakes are the price you pay for being human; repeated mistakes are the price you pay for being stubborn. So don't be hardheaded: learn from your experiences—the first time!

more stuff to think about

I hope you don't mind me telling you all this?
One can learn only by seeing one's mistakes.

C. S. Lewis

Very few things motivate us to give God our undivided attention like being faced with the negative consequences of our decisions.

Charles Stanley

The Big Idea

Fix it sooner rather than later: If you make a mistake, the time to make things better is now, not later! The sooner you admit your mistake, the better.

SELF-ESTEEM

Day 83

Form Habits That Are Pleasing to God

I the LORD search the heart and examine the mind,
to reward a man according to his conduct,
according to what his deeds deserve.

JEREMIAH 17:10 NIV

It's an old saying and a true one: First, you make your habits, and then your habits make you. Some habits will inevitably bring you closer to God; other habits will lead you away from the path He has chosen for you. If you sincerely desire to improve your spiritual health, you must honestly examine the habits that make up the fabric of your day. And you must abandon those habits that are displeasing to God.

If you trust God, and if you keep asking for His help, He can transform your life. If you sincerely ask Him to help you, the same God who created the universe will help you defeat the harmful habits that have heretofore defeated you. So, if at first you don't succeed, keep praying. God is listening, and He's ready to help you become a better person if you ask Him . . . so ask today.

2 minutes A DAY

He who does not overcome small faults,
shall fall little by little into greater ones.

THOMAS À KEMPIS

If you do not shun small defects,
bit by bit you will fall into greater ones.

THOMAS À KEMPIS

Begin to be now what you will be hereafter.

ST. JEROME

The Big Idea

First you make your habits; then your habits make you.
So, it's always a good time to think about the kind of person
your habits are making you.

SELF-ESTEEM

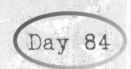

Make Up Your Mind to Be Happy Today

Whereas you do not know what will happen tomorrow.
For what is your life? It is even a vapor that appears for
a little time and then vanishes away.

JAMES 4:14 NJKV

When will you rejoice at God's marvelous creation? Today or tomorrow? When will you accept His abundance: now or later? When will you accept the peace that can and should be yours? In the present moment or in the distant future? The answer, of course, is straightforward: the best moment to accept God's gifts is the present one.

Will you accept God's blessings now or later? Are you willing to give Him your full attention today? Hopefully so. He deserves it. And so, for that matter, do you.

2 minutes a Day

more stuff to think about

Men spend their lives in anticipation, in determining to be vastly happy at some period or other, when they have time. But the present time has one advantage over every other: it is ours.

CHARLES CALEB COLTON

Life is 10% what happens to you and 90% how you respond to it.

CHARLES SWINDOLL

It's your choice: you can either count your blessings or recount your disappointments.

JIM GALLERY

The Big Idea

If you want to find lasting happiness, don't chase it. Instead, do your duty, obey your God, and wait for happiness to find you.

SELF-ESTEEM

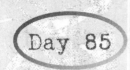

Day 85

Establish Priorities
That Please God

*And I pray this: that your love will keep on growing in
knowledge and every kind of discernment, so that you
can determine what really matters and can be pure and
blameless in the day of Christ.*

PHILIPPIANS 1:9 HOLMAN CSB

Is God a big priority for you . . . or is He an afterthought?
Do you give God your best or what's left? Have you given
Christ your heart, your soul, your talents, your time, and
your testimony? Or are you giving Him little more than a few
hours each Sunday morning?

In the book of Exodus, God warns that we should
place no gods before Him. Yet all too often, we place our
Lord in second, third, or fourth place as we worship the
gods of pride, money, or personal gratification. When we
unwittingly place possessions or relationships above our love
for the Creator, we must realign our priorities or suffer the
consequences.

Does God rule your heart? Make certain that the honest
answer to this question is a resounding yes. In the life of
every radical believer, God comes first. And that's precisely
the place that He deserves in your heart.

more stuff to think about

Like Jesus in his time on earth, you must set priorities, choose from among many good causes that vie for your attention, and seek to do what will be most effective for the advancement of God's rule.

STANLEY GRENZ

Jesus Christ is the first and last, author and finisher, beginning and end, alpha and omega, and by Him all other things hold together. He must be first or nothing. God never comes next!

VANCE HAVNER

The Big Idea

Your days are probably filled to the brim with lots of obligations. But remember: no obligation is greater than the debt you owe to your Creator. So make sure that you give Him the time He deserves, not only on Sundays, but also on every other day of the week.

SELF-ESTEEM

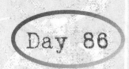

Know That Drugs Will Wreck Your Life

Be on your guard, so that your minds are not dulled from carousing, drunkenness, and worries of life.

LUKE 21:34 HOLMAN CSB

Ours is a society that glamorizes the use of drugs, alcohol, cigarettes, and other addictive substances. Why? The answer can be summed up in one word: money. Simply put, addictive substances are big money makers, so suppliers (of both legal and illegal substances) work overtime to make certain that people like you sample their products. The suppliers need a steady stream of new customers because the old ones are dying off (fast), so they engage in a no-holds-barred struggle to find new users—or more accurately, new abusers.

If you want to wreck your self-esteem—not to mention your health—allow yourself to become an addict. But if you want to enhance your sense of self-worth, treat addictive substances like life-destroying poisons that they are.

more stuff to think about

The drunken man is a living corpse.

ST. JOHN CHRYSOSTOM

Addiction is the most powerful psychic enemy
of humanity's desire for God.

GERALD MAY

The soul that journeys to God, but doesn't shake off
its cares and quiet its appetites,
is like someone who drags a cart uphill.

ST. JOHN OF THE CROSS

The Big Idea

If you're using drugs, you're risking your future and your life.
So treat illegal drugs like poison, which, by the way, they are.

SELF-ESTEEM

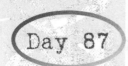

Say "No" to Things That Aren't from God

*If you're not welcomed, not listened to, quietly withdraw.
Don't make a scene. Shrug your shoulders
and be on your way.*

Mark 6:11 MSG

Sometimes, you may feel pressured to compromise yourself, and you may be afraid of what will happen if you firmly say "No." You may be afraid that you'll be rejected. But here's a tip: don't worry too much about rejection, especially when you're rejected for doing the right thing.

Pleasing other people is a good thing . . . up to a point. But you must never allow your "willingness to please" to interfere with your own good judgment or with God's commandments.

God gave you a conscience for a reason: to inform you about the difference between right and wrong. It's up to you to follow your conscience wherever it may lead, even if it means making unpopular decisions. Your job, should you choose to accept it, is to be popular with God, not people.

2 minutes a day

more stuff to think about

When you taste a measure of being able to love and enjoy the people in your life, without having to have any particular response from them, you are tasting bliss.

PAULA RINEHART

There may be no trumpet sound or loud applause when we make a right decision, just a calm sense of resolution and peace.

GLORIA GAITHER

Christians are the citizens of heaven, and while we are on earth, we ought to behave like heaven's citizens.

WARREN WIERSBE

The Big Idea

It's pretty simple: do the right thing. After all, if you're misbehaving, how can you possibly hope to feel good about yourself?

SELF-ESTEEM

Don't Whine

*Do everything readily and cheerfully—no bickering,
no second-guessing allowed! Go out into the world
uncorrupted, a breath of fresh air in this squalid and polluted
society. Provide people with a glimpse of good living and of
the living God. Carry the light-giving Message into the night.*
PHILIPPIANS 2:14-15 MSG

Because we are imperfect human beings, we often lose sight of our blessings. Ironically, most of us have more blessings than we can count, but we may still find reasons to complain about the minor frustrations of everyday life. To do so, of course, is not only wrong; it is also the pinnacle of shortsightedness and a serious roadblock on the path to spiritual abundance.

Are you tempted to complain about the inevitable minor frustrations of everyday living? Don't do it! Today and every day, make it a practice to count your blessings, not your hardships. It's the truly decent way to live.

2 minutes A DAY

more stuff to think about

The last of the human freedoms is to choose
one's attitude in any given set of circumstances.

VIKTOR FRANKL

He wants us to have a faith that does not complain
while waiting, but rejoices because we know our times
are in His hands—nail-scarred hands that labor
for our highest good.

KAY ARTHUR

Jesus wept, but he never complained.

C. H. SPURGEON

The Big Idea

Perpetual complaining is a bad habit, and it's contagious
. . . make sure that your family members don't catch it from
you!

SELF-ESTEEM

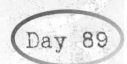

Give God Your Complete Attention

Worship the Lord your God and . . . serve Him only.
MATTHEW 4:10 HOLMAN CSB

Nineteenth-century clergyman Edwin Hubbel Chapin warned, "Neutral men are the devil's allies." His words were true then, and they're true now. Neutrality in the face of evil is a sin. Yet all too often, we fail to fight evil, not because we are neutral, but because we are shortsighted: we don't fight the devil because we don't recognize his handiwork.

If we are to recognize evil and fight it, we must pay careful attention. We must pay attention to God's Word, and we must pay attention to the realities of everyday life. When we observe life objectively, and when we do so with eyes and hearts that are attuned to God's Holy Word, we can no longer be neutral believers. And when we are no longer neutral, God rejoices while the devil despairs.

more stuff to think about

The greatest enemy of holiness is not passion; it is apathy.

JOHN ELDREDGE

As we find that it is not easy to persevere in this being "alone with God," we begin to realize that it is because we are not "wholly for God." God has a right to demand that He should have us completely for Himself.

ANDREW MURRAY

I need the spiritual revival that comes from spending quiet time alone with Jesus in prayer and in thoughtful meditation on His Word.

ANNE GRAHAM LOTZ

The Big Idea

Sometimes (but not always) our difficult circumstances are God's way of getting our attention or correcting our behavior. So here's an important question: Is God trying to get your attention today?

SELF-ESTEEM

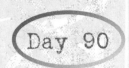

Day 90

Make God's Word Your Roadmap

Teach me, O LORD, the way of Your statutes,
and I shall keep it to the end.
PSALM 119:33 NKJV

As you look to the future and decide upon the direction of your life, what will you use as your roadmap? Will you trust God's Holy Word and use it as an indispensable tool to guide your steps? Or will you choose a different map to guide your steps? The map you choose will determine the quality of your journey and its ultimate destination.

The Bible is the ultimate guide for life; make it your guidebook as well. When you do, you can be comforted in the knowledge that your steps are guided by a Source of wisdom and truth that never fails.

more stuff to think about

The Bible was not given to increase our knowledge
but to change our lives.

D. L. MOODY

The Bible is a Christian's guidebook, and I believe the
knowledge it sheds on pain and suffering is the great
antidote to fear for suffering people.
Knowledge can dissolve fear as light destroys darkness.

PHILIP YANCEY

We don't have loose-leaf Bibles.
We can't just open the binding and take out
what we don't want to do or to believe.

ROBERT SUGGS

The Big Idea

It's up to you: nobody can study the Bible for you . . .
you've got to study it for yourself. And that's exactly what you
should do.

SELF-ESTEEM

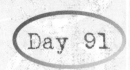

Day 91

Seek Fellowship

*Then all the people went away to eat and drink, to send
some of their food to others, and to celebrate with great joy.
They finally understood what they had been taught.*

NEHEMIAH 8:12 NCV

Fellowship with other believers should be an integral
part of your everyday life. Your association with
fellow Christians should be uplifting, enlightening,
encouraging, and consistent.

Are you an active member of your own fellowship?
Are you a builder of bridges inside the four walls of your
church and outside it? Do you contribute to God's glory by
contributing your time and your talents to a close-knit band
of believers? Hopefully so. The fellowship of believers is
intended to be a powerful tool for spreading God's Good
News and uplifting His children. And God intends that you
be a fully contributing member of that fellowship. Your
intentions should be the same.

2 MINUTES A DAY

more stuff to think about

One of the ways God refills us after failure is through the blessing of Christian fellowship. Just experiencing the joy of simple activities shared with other children of God can have a healing effect on us.

ANNE GRAHAM LOTZ

The Bible knows nothing of solitary religion.

JOHN WESLEY

Christians are like coals of a fire. Together they glow— apart they grow cold.

ANONYMOUS

The Big Idea

Christians shouldn't try to be Lone Rangers. We are members of a spiritual family, and we need one another. Are you trying to be a Lone Ranger? If so, it's time to form a posse made up of faithful, God-fearing friends.

SELF-ESTEEM

Remember That You Are Unique

For you made us only a little lower than God,
and you crowned us with glory and honor.

PSALM 8:5 NLT

The only person in the world who's exactly like you . . . IS YOU! And that means you're special: special to God, special to your family, special to your friends, and a special addition to God's wonderful world!

But sometimes, when you're tired, angry, dejected, or depressed, you may not feel very special. In fact, you may decide that you're the ugliest duckling in the pond, a not-very-special person . . . but whenever you think like that, you're mistaken.

The Bible says that God made you in "an amazing and wonderful way." So the next time that you start feeling like you don't measure up, remember this: when God made all the people of the earth, He only made one you. You're incredibly valuable to God, and that means that you should think of yourself as a V.I.P. God wants you to have the best, and you deserve the best . . . you're worth it!

more stuff to think about

You're the only one who can do what you do.

LOIS EVANS

The splendor of the rose and the whiteness of the lily
do not rob the little violet of its scent nor the daisy
of its simple charm. If every tiny flower wanted to be a rose,
spring would lose its loveliness.

THÉRÈSE OF LISIEUX

The Big Idea

You are unique. Do you think of yourself that way? If so,
congratulations. If not, why not?

SELF-ESTEEM

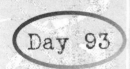

Day 93

Keep Life in Perspective

He will teach us His ways, and we shall walk in His paths.
ISAIAH 2:3 NKJV

For most of us, life is busy and complicated. Amid the rush and crush of the daily grind, it is easy to lose perspective . . . easy, but wrong. When our world seems to be spinning out of control, we must simply seek to regain perspective by slowing ourselves down and then turning our thoughts and prayers toward God.

The familiar words of Psalm 46:10 remind us to "Be still, and know that I am God" (NKJV). When we do so, we encounter the awesome presence of our loving Heavenly Father, and we are blessed beyond words. But, when we ignore the presence of our Creator, we rob ourselves of His perspective, His peace, and His joy.

Today and every day, set aside a time to be still before God. When you do, you'll feel better about your life, your future, and your Creator—and you can face the day's complications with the wisdom and power that only God can provide.

2 MINUTES A DAY

more stuff to think about

When considering the size of your problems, there are two categories that you should never worry about: the problems that are small enough for you to handle, and the ones that aren't too big for God to handle.

MARIE T. FREEMAN

As I contemplate all the sacrifices required in order to live a life that is totally focused on Jesus Christ and His eternal kingdom, the joy seeps out of my heart onto my face in a smile of deep satisfaction.

ANNE GRAHAM LOTZ

Life is a masterpiece in the making. And if your perspective is true, the whole canvas will be beautiful.

THOMAS KINKADE

The Big Idea

Your life is a priceless gift from God. Spend time each day thanking God for that gift.

SELF-ESTEEM

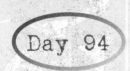

Steer Clear
of the Road to Ruin

Don't turn off the road of goodness;
keep away from evil paths.

PROVERBS 4:27 NCV

How hard is it to bump into temptation in this crazy world? Not very hard. The devil, it seems, is causing pain and heartache in more places and in more ways than ever before. We, as Christians, must remain vigilant. Not only must we resist Satan when he confronts us, but we must also avoid those places where Satan can most easily tempt us. And, if we are to avoid the unending temptations of this world, we must earnestly wrap ourselves in the protection of God's Holy Word.

The road to ruin is wide, long, and deadly. Avoid it, and help others do the same. When you do, God will smile—and the devil won't.

more stuff to think about

Good and evil both increase at compound interest.
That is why the little decisions you and I make every day
are of such infinite importance.

C. S. Lewis

Never be afraid of the world's censure;
it's praise is much more to be dreaded.

C. H. Spurgeon

If the cost of popularity is too high,
you're better off being anonymous.

Criswell Freeman

The Big Idea

Here in the 21st century, the road to ruin is big, fast, wide,
and crowded. Steer clear.

SELF-ESTEEM

A Faith Bigger Than Fear

Do not let your hearts be troubled. Trust in God;
trust also in me. In my Father's house are many rooms;
if it were not so, I would have told you. I am going there to
prepare a place for you.

JOHN 14:1-2 NIV

American clergyman Edward Everett Hale observed, "Some people bear three kinds of trouble—the ones they've had, the ones they have, and the ones they expect to have." How true. But a better strategy for you is this: accept the past, live in the present, and place the future in God's capable hands.

As you face the challenges of everyday life, you may be comforted by this fact: Trouble, of every kind, is temporary. Yet, God's grace is eternal. And worries, of every kind, are temporary. But God's love is everlasting. The troubles that concern you will pass. God remains. And with these thoughts in mind, it's now time for you to place today's troubles in their proper perspective.

2 MINUTES A DAY

more stuff to think about

Worry and anxiety are sand in the machinery of life;
faith is the oil.

E. Stanley Jones

Nothing true or beautiful or good makes complete sense in
any immediate context of history;
therefore we must be saved by faith.

Reinhold Neibuhr

I want my life to be a faith-filled leap into his arms, knowing
he will be there—not that everything will go as I want,
but that he will be there and that this will be enough.

Sheila Walsh

The Big Idea

Are you feeling anxious or fearful? If so, trust God to handle
those problems that are simply too big for you to solve.
Entrust the future—your future—to God.

SELF-ESTEEM

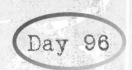

Keep Following
in His Footsteps

*But whoever keeps His word, truly in him the love of God is
perfected. This is how we know we are in Him: the one who
says he remains in Him should walk just as He walked.*

1 JOHN 2:5-6 HOLMAN CSB

L ife is a series of decisions and choices. Each day, we
make countless decisions that can bring us closer to
God . . . or not. When we live according to God's
commandments, we reap bountiful rewards: abundance,
hope, and peace, for starters. But, when we turn our backs
upon God by disobeying Him, we bring needless suffering
upon ourselves and our families.

Do you seek to walk in the footsteps of the One from
Galilee, or will you choose another path? If you sincerely
seek God's peace and His blessings, then you must strive to
imitate God's Son.

Thomas Brooks spoke for believers of every generation
when he observed, "Christ is the sun, and all the watches
of our lives should be set by the dial of his motion." Christ,
indeed, is the ultimate Savior of mankind and the personal
Savior of those who believe in Him. As His servants, we
should walk in His footsteps as we share His love and His
message with a world that needs both.

more stuff to think about

If you are looking for the way by which you should go,
take Christ, for he is himself the way.

THOMAS AQUINAS

Jesus never asks us to give Him what we don't have.
But He does demand that we give Him all we do have
if we want to be a part of what He wishes to do in the lives
of those around us!

ANNE GRAHAM LOTZ

We have in Jesus Christ a perfect example of how to put
God's truth into practice.

BILL BRIGHT

The Big Idea

You don't have to be perfect to follow in Christ's footsteps.
Jesus doesn't expect your perfection—He expects your
participation.

SELF-ESTEEM

Don't Enter Popularity Contests

*Do you think I am trying to make people accept me?
No, God is the One I am trying to please. Am I trying to
please people? If I still wanted to please people,
I would not be a servant of Christ.*

GALATIANS 1:10 NCV

Are you a people-pleaser or a God-pleaser? Hopefully, you're far more concerned with pleasing God than you are with pleasing your friends. But face facts: even if you're a devoted Christian, you're still going to feel the urge to impress your friends and acquaintances—and sometimes that urge will be strong.

Peer pressure can be good or bad, depending upon who your peers are and how they behave. If your friends encourage you to follow God's will and to obey His commandments, then you'll experience positive peer pressure, and that's a good thing. But, if your friends encourage you to do foolish things, then you're facing a different kind of peer pressure . . . and you'd better beware.

To sum it up, here's your choice: you can choose to please God first, or you can fall victim to peer pressure. The choice is yours—and so are the consequences.

2 Minutes A Day

more stuff to think about

Long ago I ceased to count heads.
Truth is often in the minority in this evil world.

C. H. Spurgeon

Lord, I am no longer my own, but Yours. Put me to what You
will, rank me with whom You will. Let me be employed by
You or laid aside for You, exalted for You or brought low by
You. Let me have all things, let me have nothing. I freely and
heartily yield all things to Your pleasure and disposal.
And now, O glorious and blessed God, Father, Son, and
Holy Spirit, You are mine and I am Yours. So be it. Amen.

John Wesley

The Big Idea

If you're overly concerned about being "popular," ask
yourself these three questions:

1. Why am I trying so hard to please everybody?
2. How often do I compromise my principles in order to gain
popularity?
3. Is God concerned about my being "popular," or is He
more concerned about my obedience to Him?

SELF-ESTEEM

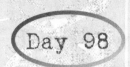

Let God Transform Your Life

*Your old life is dead. Your new life, which is your real life—
even though invisible to spectators—is with Christ in God.
He is your life.*

Colossians 3:3 MSG

Has your relationship with Jesus transformed you into an extremely different person? Hopefully so! Otherwise, you're missing out on the joy and abundance that can be yours through Christ.

Think, for a moment, about the "old" you, the person you were before you invited Christ to reign over your heart. Now, think about the "new" you, the person you've become since then. Is there a difference between the "old" version of you and the "new-and-improved" version? There should be! And that difference should be evident to you, to your family, and to your friends.

When you invited Christ to reign over your heart, you became a radically new creation. This day offers yet another opportunity to behave yourself like that new person. When you do, God will guide your steps and bless your endeavors . . . forever.

Are you willing to make radical changes for Jesus? If so, you may be certain of this fact: He's standing at the door of your heart, patiently waiting to form an extreme, life-altering relationship with you.

more stuff to think about

Believe and do what God says. The life-changing consequences will be limitless, and the results will be confidence and peace of mind.

FRANKLIN GRAHAM

God has sent His Holy Spirit to transform us into more accurate reflections of who God is....

BILL HYBELS

God's work is not in buildings, but in transformed lives.

RUTH BELL GRAHAM

The Big Idea

A true conversion experience results in a life transformed by Christ and a commitment to following in His footsteps.

SELF-ESTEEM

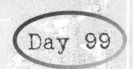

Meet with God Every Morning

Every morning he wakes me. He teaches me to listen like a student. The Lord God helps me learn . . . .
Isaiah 50:4-5 NCV

Do you have a standing appointment with God every morning? Is God your first priority, or do you talk with Him less frequently than that?" If you're wise, you'll talk to God first thing every day, without exception.

Warren Wiersbe writes, "Surrender your mind to the Lord at the beginning of each day." And that's sound advice. When you begin each day with your head bowed and your heart lifted, you are reminded of God's love, His protection, and His commandments. Then, you can align your priorities for the coming day with the teachings and commandments that God has placed upon your heart.

So, if you've acquired the unfortunate habit of trying to "squeeze" God into the corners of your life, it's time to reshuffle the items on your to-do list by placing God first. And if you haven't already done so, form the habit of spending quality time each morning with your Creator. He deserves it . . . and so, for that matter, do you.

more stuff to think about

Ten minutes spent in Christ's society every day,
aye two minutes, will make the whole day different.

HENRY DRUMMOND

Whatever is your best time in the day,
give that to communion with God.

HUDSON TAYLOR

Be still, and in the quiet moments, listen to the voice of your
heavenly Father. His words can renew your spirit—
no one knows you and your needs like He does.

JANET L. WEAVER SMITH

The Big Idea

Make an appointment with God and keep it. Bible study and
prayer should be at the top of your to-do list, not the bottom.

SELF-ESTEEM

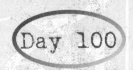

Remember God's Promise
of Eternal Life

For God so loved the world that he gave his only Son,
so that everyone who believes in him will not perish
but have eternal life.

JOHN 3:16 NLT

Okay, we've come to the end of our 100-day discussion about building your sense of self-worth. Let's conclude by talking, once again, about the ultimate form of self-respect: your decision to establish an eternal relationship with Jesus Christ.

Eternal life is not an event that begins when you die. Eternal life begins when you invite Jesus into your heart right here on earth. So, it's important to remember that God's plans for you are not limited to the ups and downs of everyday life. If you've allowed Jesus to reign over your heart, you've already begun your eternal journey.

Today, give praise to the Creator for His priceless gift, the gift of eternal life. And then, when you've offered Him your thanks and your praise, share His Good News with all who cross your path.

more stuff to think about

Someday you will read in the papers that Moody is dead.
Don't you believe a word of it. At that moment I shall be
more alive than I am now. I was born of the flesh in 1837,
I was born of the spirit in 1855. That which is born of
the flesh may die. That which is born of the
Spirit shall live forever.

D. L. MOODY

Once a man is united to God, how could he not live
forever? Once a man is separated from God,
what can he do but wither and die?

C. S. LEWIS

Christ is the only liberator whose liberation lasts forever.

MALCOLM MUGGERIDGE

The Big Idea

People love talking about religion, and everybody has their
own opinions, but ultimately only one opinion counts . . .
God's. Think about God's promise of eternal life—and what
that promise means to you.

SELF-ESTEEM